LYNNE LUMLEY

A GOOD ENOUGH MOTHER

The 7 Step Formula
to Let Go of Guilt
and Trust Your
Parenting Skills

WHY NOT HAVE LYNNE LUMLEY AS A GUEST SPEAKER ON YOUR PODCAST, SEMINAR, FESTIVAL OR EVENT?

www.agoodenoughmother.com | www.phoenixhypnotherapy.com.au

Tel: +61 438 411 551
Email: lynne@phoenixhypnotherapy.com.au   **Email:** lynne@agoodenoughmother.com
Website: www.phoenixhypnotherapy.com.au

This is a callout to all mothers, stepmothers, and grandmothers who love unconditionally. If you've ever battled with mother's guilt or wondered if you've done enough, then Lynne will inspire and uplift you to let go of Mother's guilt and trust in your parenting skills.

Lynne Lumley understands motherhood from many perspectives:

- As a proud mother of four, a stepmother to three amazing children and a Nonna to two scrumptious bundles of joy.
- And as a psychotherapist and clinical hypnotherapist specialising in helping mums know that they are good enough.

There were times when Lynne wondered whether she was good enough. She spent years in a desperate fight for her daughter's life and shares an incredible journey of survival that inspires and uplifts audiences around the globe. Lynne shares her wisdom and step-by-step strategies in the hope that other mums connect with their intuition to embrace the best version of themselves, both as mothers and as beautiful, vibrant, and astounding women too.

BOOKS BY LYNNE LUMLEY

A GOOD ENOUGH MOTHER
The 7 Step Formula to Let Go of Guilt and Trust Your Parenting Skills

This is an essential book to discover how to recognise and let go of lingering guilts, blames, or shames that interfere with your relationship with your children. Uncover strengths you've hoped were there and the confidence to tap into your intuition and parenting skills. The author helps you come to a peaceful understanding that you are *a good enough mother*.

CONNECT WITH LYNNE LUMLEY ON FACEBOOK
https://www.facebook.com/agoodenoughmother/

Download free resources from A Good Enough Mother
www.agoodenoughmother.com/resources

LYNNE LUMLEY

A GOOD ENOUGH MOTHER

The 7 Step Formula to Let Go of Guilt and Trust Your Parenting Skills

The Potentialist
by Maggie White

Mind Potential Publishing

Copyright © 2020 Lynne Lumley and Phoenix Hypnotherapy

ALL RIGHTS RESERVED. No part of this book may be reproduced or transmitted in any form whatsoever, electronic, or mechanical, including photocopying, recording, or by any informational storage or retrieval system without the expressed written permission from the author and publisher.

Author: Lynne Lumley
Title: A Good Enough Mother
ISBN Paperback: 978-1-922380-09-8
ISBN Kindle: 978-1-922380-11-1

 A catalogue record for this book is available from the National Library of Australia

Category: Self Help Techniques | Family

Publisher: Mind Potential Publishing
Division of Mind Design Centre Pty Ltd, PO Box 6094, Maroochydore BC Queensland, Australia, 4558.
International Phone: +61 405 138 567
Australia Phone: 1300 664 544
www.thepotentialist.com | www.agoodenoughmother.com

Cover design by Olivia Henry

Registered with the National Library

LIMITS OF LIABILITY | DISCLAIMER OF WARRANTY: The author and publisher of this book have used their best efforts in preparing this material and they disclaim any warranties, (expressed or implied) for any particular purpose. The information presented in this publication is compiled from sources believed to be accurate at the time of printing, however the publisher assumes no responsibility for omissions or errors. The author and publisher shall not be held liable for any loss or other damages, including, but not limited to incidental, consequential, or any other. This publication is not intended to replace or substitute medical or professional advice, the author and publisher disclaim any liability, loss or risk incurred as a direct or indirect consequence of the use of any content.

Where the author has mentioned specific true story case studies (other than her family members) the names and identifying details have been changed to protect the privacy of those concerned.

Mind Potential Publishing bears no responsibility for the accuracy of the information provided as either online or offline links contained in this publication. The use of links to websites does not constitute an endorsement by the publisher. The publisher assumes no liability for content or opinion expressed by the author. Opinions expressed by the Author do not represent the opinion of Mind Potential Publishing or Mind Design Centre Pty Ltd.

Printed in Australia

DEDICATION

This book is dedicated to so many for their love, support and encouragement to finally write this book. It's been a long time coming.

Firstly, and the core reason I had the courage to write this book, my hero, Gabrielle. My darling Gabby, your courage and innate fighter's spirit to survive and to demand you were heard through the diversity of your illness, continues to inspire and move me forward.

To my three other extraordinary children Sarah, Kieran and Ebony. I am blessed to have the opportunity to be loved and cherished by you. I am forever thankful for the gift of being your mum and to learn and be inspired by your strengths and achievements and most of all, the depths of your hearts.

To my wonderful stepsons; Kevin, Adam and Nicholas, thank you for welcoming me into your hearts and for the great 'Brady Bunch' gatherings of laughter and joy.

To my mum Gwenny, who taught me to have faith and belief in myself, to appreciate that simplicity in life can bring the most joy, and to love unconditionally.

To my ever-enduring husband Shane, who supports, loves and encourages me each and every day.

Last but not least, to the other mothers, grandmothers, stepmothers who love unconditionally. I honour you!

CONTENTS

Foreword	1
Introduction	3
Chapter 1: A Mother's Story	9
Chapter 2: Let Go of Guilt – the Mistakes We Make as Parents	27
Chapter 3: Near Enough Has to Be Good Enough	39
Chapter 4: When I Can't Fix Everything	49
Chapter 5: When Change Happens	57
Chapter 6: Time for Me, Time for Them	69
Chapter 7: The Brady Bunch Myth – When Two Families Become One	81
Chapter 8: Who's the Adult Here?	95
You ARE a Good Enough Mother	107
Acknowledgments	123
Meet the Contributors	125
References and Recommended Reading	127
Meet the Author	133
The Family Gallery	135
What Others Have to Say	139

FOREWORD

Lynne writes powerfully about her experiences in the thick of working mother chaos. We can all relate to her hilarious account of a morning routine that involves throwing on clothes while the children eat carbonised bacon to the tune of a fire alarm. Her now adult children are a credit to her "Good Enough" mothering.

They are a tight knit bunch of accomplished, resilient and altruistic young people. Without her tireless advocacy and tenacious search for answers, her daughter, Gabby, may well have died of her illness.

Lynne's indefatigable support for her daughter did indeed make her "That Mum" in the eyes of some health care workers. However, it's up to us as health care workers to listen and act when a mother's intuition says their child needs help.

Because of Lynne's tireless work, her daughter became the first in Australia to receive state of the art rehabilitation for Rumination Syndrome. Since then, Lynne has helped countless others by being "That Mum" and that is definitely "Good Enough"!

Dr Frances Connor
Paediatric Gastroenterologist

INTRODUCTION

This is a story about one mother's fight, and yet this is a story that all mothers can relate to.

This is a story for every mother, stepmother or grandmother who wakes at night in turmoil, who questions whether she is doing this 'mother thing' right. Or wonders whether she is good enough; searching for the answers, agonising over choices, opinions and information, in order to make the right decisions for their children.

This is a story for every mother who has ever wondered – am I doing this parenting thing right?

The telling of this very personal journey is for mothers who want a closer, guilt-free relationship with their children, no matter what age – you deserve to know you are the very best mother you can be.

I invite you to be brave and courageous throughout this book, to learn from my mistakes as a mother who is willing to admit I often got it wrong.

I invite you to trust that you are the perfect mother for your children, even while you discover how to be a better version of

INTRODUCTION

yourself. To know that any hardship is an opportunity to grow, learn, evolve and strengthen the connection within your family and the bond between a mother and her children.

In Chapter 1 you'll get to know my story as a mother, the battles I went through, and the guilt I suffered. It's the story of how my daughter ended up in a high security mental ward, even though I knew there was nothing psychologically wrong with her. She had a physical condition, but it took years to discover what it was and how to treat it. In the meantime, my beautiful daughter suffered terribly, both physically and emotionally.

For many years after Gabby stabilised, even long after I had eventually found the truth that saved her life, I still wondered if I was a good enough mother. *"How could I have let her suffer the horrors she went through?"*

What I had to learn, in order to trust my parenting skills again, was to release my guilt and to know that I really am a good enough mother. It's the reason I knew I had to write this book.

Today I know I AM a good enough mother.

No-one can break that connection between Gabby and me anymore. We are strong and she is alive, vibrant and a force to be reckoned with. She is my inspiration. No-one will ever make me doubt my mother's intuition.

I trust myself as a parent. The relationship with my daughter and all of my children is united and strong.

My hope for you is this book will help you find that place of knowing too. To know beyond simply words that you are a good enough mother.

Yes, we all make mistakes, and it is from these mistakes that we learn and become better.

Hanging on to guilt and doubt as a parent, only serves to hinder and get in the way of the bond with our children. It eats away and serves no purpose.

Throughout this book, my hope is that you'll come with me on a journey to release any lingering guilts, blames or shames that have interfered or are currently interfering with your relationship with your children. To trust and tap into your intuition, and to come to a peaceful understanding that you are…

A GOOD ENOUGH MOTHER

I'll do this with step-by-step answers to your questions, guidance as a therapist using my 7 Step Formula to let go of guilt and tap into your *inner knowing*. And, importantly, I'll do this as a mother, a stepmother, as a grandmother and as a daughter too. I'll guide you through the steps to let go of the guilt and trust your parenting skills so that you can feel safe to step into the true connection of motherhood and deepen your bond with your children too.

Throughout the book, I have drawn upon my personal family experiences, those of my clients who have been willing to share their stories, and my wealth of experience as a clinical therapist to guide you through the steps that will help you recognise and release the guilt that holds you back as a parent.

I will walk you through my 7 Step Formula to clear the channels between the real, mother's guilt and how you think and feel about:

1. What has or hasn't happened
2. What you did or didn't do
3. What you could have or shouldn't have said and
4. All you wished you'd done differently

I do this so that the connection to your inner voice, your knowledge as a mother and as a beautiful woman, strengthens and shines from within.

INTRODUCTION

The 7 Step Formula will be explained in detail throughout the book and used as an easy system to let go of any lingering challenges with guilt and trust your mother's intuition.

From one mother to another, I understand how motherhood can be both challenging one minute and so delicious the next!

Lynne x

*A mothers instincts
are amazing.
Trust those instincts.
They can tell you
what to do
long before your head
can figure it out.*

CHAPTER 1
A Mother's Story

My heart broke, I felt like I was abandoning her, locking her up and leaving her in jail.

My daughter Gabby was screaming and begging me, "Don't leave me Mummy! Don't leave me here." Each agonising cry shattered what was left of my certainty. Doubts flooded back to my mind, was I doing the right thing for my baby girl?

In one moment, the years of doubt that had led to this point, flooded my mind and added to my guilt at not knowing what else to do. *"Please, Please, PLEEAASSEE... Mummy! Don't leave me here!"*

The hardest thing I've ever had to do as a mother, or in fact in my entire life, was to leave my beautiful girl locked and alone, in a secure high-level mental ward.

It was 2012, Gabby was gravely ill, and only 14 years old.

I'd run out of choices and had nowhere to turn. The doctors told me they were extremely concerned for her life and that this was the only option I had.

CHAPTER 1: A MOTHER'S STORY

I remember my thoughts screaming inside, "You have got to be kidding. I'm her mother, I am more than concerned for her, I am desperate to know what to do to protect Gabby and save her life."

That was why we were now standing in this high-security mental ward, it was our last resort, we were begging for someone to help her.

In the years leading up to this moment, I had tried everything I knew. The past seven years had been spent researching, testing and fighting to find out what was physically wrong with my child. Gabby had faded before our eyes, and nothing I had done so far had worked. Nothing I had researched had made any difference. Her health had continued to decline. Her blood results had continued to show a child barely holding onto life. And now we were here… at this point, with what felt like no other choice.

I was terrified I would lose her, so fearful that her heart would just stop.

The latest tests had revealed that her potassium levels were dangerously low, and this had put her heart at risk. My beautiful girl was a fighter, and I simply didn't know what else to do, where else to turn.

The one thing I was put on this earth to do was to keep my children safe, and for Gabby, it felt like I was failing.

As I turned to walk away, the sound of Gabby's pleading in the distance was like a knife to my heart. I was sobbing uncontrollably too. My heart, already broken, was now shattered. "What good am I if I can't keep my baby safe, if I can't care for my own daughter?"

If I only knew then, what I know now!

I was at a complete loss. I was empty. I had become exhausted by the fight. I trusted the medical team, and I was no longer listening to my inner knowing. I'd lost faith in myself and that inner guidance that had kept me strong until now. I had listened to my intuition before and look what that had achieved for Gabby. I really didn't know what to do anymore. I'd begun to believe what the medical team kept telling me. It was like they knew my daughter better than I did. Like they knew her better than she did herself.

When I think back to that day, many years ago now, I have glimpses of how deeply I felt the sense of failure as a mother. In that moment I was wracked with guilt and doubt. I was too scared to take her home, because the medical team would not help her if I did. They had threatened that if I didn't leave her with them in the mental ward, she could die.

The team kept insisting they knew how to help her and that whatever was happening to Gabby was all psychological. According to them her sickness was self-imposed. If I dared take her home with me, I was terrified they'd have the police knocking on my door to take her away.

I know now that fear and helplessness got in the way of certainty and intuition. I didn't do what I knew was right for my daughter. If only I knew what I know now…to trust my own strengths as a mother.

Before I go any further, I want to reassure you that there really are happy endings.

Just the other day, as Gabby and I were training in Muay Thai together, I watched her healthy, strong body as she kicked and put her full force into the pads. I'm so thankful she has come through this and is still the fighter she has always been.

In hindsight, the two of us became completely united in the fight to uncover a real diagnosis for her condition. We connected in the fight to eventually get her released from the mental ward and find the actual path she needed, to help her body find health again. We became fearless and unstoppable.

No matter how much we pleaded with the medical team that this illness was physical, not mental, not one person back then believed either of us. No matter how many times Gabby insisted she was not doing this to herself, they didn't listen to, or believe, either of us.

The medical team insisted that Gabby was starving herself to death. That she was eating food, then purging on purpose.

I knew my daughter. I knew she was not purging herself of food as part of a need for control. I knew these symptoms were spontaneous, automated in fact. I knew with certainty that her body was unconsciously and spontaneously rejecting food. It wasn't Gabby doing that to herself, it was her body fighting some other unknown demon that no medical team we'd met so far was willing to investigate.

But I allowed my overwhelm of not knowing what else to do get in the way of the truth.

Her body was wasting away, she'd become incapable of keeping food down and had become so depleted of nutrients and potassium that she'd been hospitalised. No one believed her, or me, not one medical team member looked beyond a diagnosis of a suspected eating disorder. They openly accused Gabby of purging, bulimia and potential anorexia. Their refusal to delve deeper risked my daughter's life even further.

I remember asking repeatedly, if anyone on the medical or nursing team had ever seen this before, this involuntary regurgitation of every morsel Gabby ate and drank. Their response was always, "It's complicated." What I now know for certain is, they just didn't know and weren't willing to look beyond the easiest diagnosis.

After years of searching for the correct answer, years of poking and prodding, the medical team had deemed Gabby to be 'untrustworthy' with food. That she was actually doing this to herself.

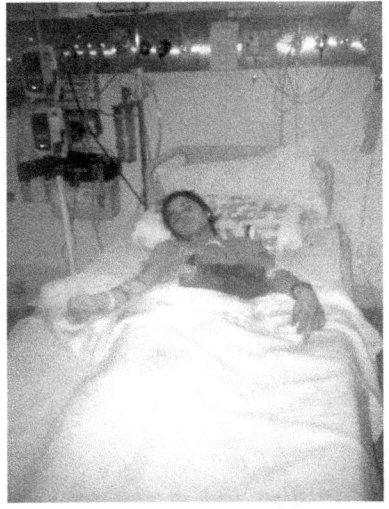
Gabby in hospital

On that fateful day, when they insisted I leave her there, I was broken. I was helpless. My power had been stripped away. She had become so deathly ill, I really believed what they told me, that she would only survive if I signed her into that ward and left her with them. They were wrong, they were so very wrong!

Life before that fateful day

Long before Gabby was born, I already had an established family of three beautiful children. Gabby was a complete surprise. When I found out I was six weeks pregnant with her, I couldn't believe it, and she has continued to surprise me ever since. This strong, talented, athletic, beautiful child called Gabrielle, (later to be lovingly known as Gabby), lived her life daringly, and she was spectacular.

I remember a camping holiday our family had in Yamba, New South Wales. We'd taken a break for a couple of weeks and were enjoying the relaxed, family atmosphere. Gabby had the freedom she wanted and would happily cycle throughout the other campers' sites on her pushbike. She was two and a half years old, and she told me in no uncertain terms that she was ready to be rid of the annoying training wheels.

CHAPTER 1: A MOTHER'S STORY

"I can ride mummy," she assured me.

I was committed to allowing all of my children to have a say in what they wanted and felt ready to experience. I was dedicated to helping them trust themselves too, and so, those training wheels were removed and away she went.

I ran alongside her until I could no longer keep up. She confidently rode ahead, riding as fast as she could, turning with skill and expertise until she did the lap and caught up with me again, only to pass me with a giggle of joy. She continued riding around that camping park, lapping me again and again.

I laugh as I write this. Gabby has continued to amaze me ever since. Riding ahead of me throughout life. Later that night, as I sat under the stars with a nice chardonnay watching the glee and camaraderie of these four wonderful children, I remember feeling so proud of them all. I remembered thinking how thankful I was that they were my children.

In that moment, I knew that I was doing a great job. I was a good mum. I remember thinking, "Just look at this gorgeously happy and healthy tribe of mine."

Healthy, happy kids

Long before Gabby was sick, she was a high achiever. She was an accomplished martial artist. Karate was her absolute love and passion and she was having a wonderful time learning and competing. When she was eight years old and about to compete at a karate tournament, she contracted a normal childhood tummy bug. After three days of being at home with me, she started to feel better, but was still regurgitating small pieces of partially digested food. My instincts knew something was wrong.

The doctor told me he had no idea what was going on but prescribed some medication to help stop the vomiting. Soon she was well enough to go back to school and continue her training and competing in martial arts. She loved every moment of it.

We went on with our lives, yet this spontaneous regurgitation continued to pop up at the most random times. Sometimes if she was ill, sometimes not.

Gabby's interest in martial arts increased and soon she was training and competing in both Karate and Muay Thai. She trained six days a week whether the vomiting was happening or not. She displayed true determination and commitment.

As a mother, I'd ask her to rest, but she was so committed to her goals that she managed her health and life around this strange condition. All this time I was taking her to a medical doctor as well as allied health professionals, but to no avail. No-one seemed to know what was going on or how to help Gabby's body stop rejecting food.

On Anzac Day, 2010 Gabby was weak from a long period of vomiting, so I took her to the doctor once again. He ran blood tests and found her potassium was dangerously low. We raced her to Brisbane Mater Children's emergency ward and she was admitted to the cardiac ward to undergo extensive tests. After a week of invasive testing, having blood taken daily and continuous cannulas and further poking and prodding, the head of paediatrics told us, "It is psychological." He said, "There's nothing we can do to help." He promptly discharged Gabby and left us with more questions than we'd had when we first arrived.

We were in shock. Gabby was still so ill. She said to the paediatrician, "I've done everything you've wanted me to do and

CHAPTER 1: A MOTHER'S STORY

you are kicking me out?" Gabby was heartbroken, and I was very scared for my baby girl.

No-one seemed to want to take us seriously, and no-one was willing to investigate further. Even leading paediatricians were happy to accept the easy explanation, leaving us high and dry with no solution and a very sick girl.

I pushed Gabby to the car in a wheelchair. She was unable to walk without almost passing out because she was so weak. I was lost, but still believing, *"I will find an answer, I just have to keep searching. I'll have to try harder."*

Things just got worse from there.

By this stage Gabby was 13 years old and had become desperately ill. She needed regular infusions to boost her potassium levels (constant vomiting results in losing a lot of potassium and electrolytes). Humans require potassium levels to be between 3.5 to 5 mmol/L in order for our hearts to function properly. Gabby's levels would drop suddenly to as low as 1.2.

Days, weeks, months rolled by with daily blood tests, rushing to emergency wards across Brisbane, band-aid medication, and cannulas to infuse potassium to keep her heart beating. Still there had been no official diagnosis, no hint at what was wrong or how to treat the cause. Instead there were continual insinuations that Gabby was doing this to herself, that it was psychological.

One particular visit to our local hospital emergency ward (to have yet another cannula to infuse potassium), Gabby was admitted again to the same children's ward. A week of ill-prepared medical support led to the medical team's belief that this was a 'complicated' eating disorder, one they had never seen before.

Unknown to me, our family general practitioner, who hadn't known how to diagnose or treat Gabby over the previous years, had decided the only cause must be that something was going on in the family home. He communicated his concerns with this new medical team, who then proceeded to call Child and Youth Mental Health Service (CYMHS).

Gabby was assessed and we were called in for a meeting in front of a board of eight clinicians.

We were told that the medical team at the Children's Hospital was not equipped to help Gabby, and they were transferring her to another facility, the Logan Hospital, Adolescent Mental Health Ward.

I pleaded with them to not isolate Gabby by sending her further away. She had wonderful siblings, step siblings and the support of friends through the Karate club community. We were told that Gabby wouldn't be able to have visitors or any outside support during her time there. They had no consideration for how important her brothers and sisters were to Gabby, and how having the support of her Karate community had provided her with strength and hope. The team made it very clear that this isolation was necessary for Gabby's safety, no matter what.

That was the day I lost my ability to advocate for my daughter.

I surrendered to their expertise and relinquished any trust I had in myself as a mother. I had no other idea of how to help my beautiful child. They were insistent they knew how to treat her, they insisted this was the best, and only way to save her life.

She was taken in the dead of night in an ambulance…

I followed scared, yet hopeful in my car…

CHAPTER 1: A MOTHER'S STORY

She was admitted through emergency and wheeled down through the silent halls, through one after another security doors, each door closing ominously behind us.

I tried to keep things light for Gabby. I reassured her, saying "It's like that TV show *Get Smart* with all the doors closing one by one behind us!"

Every part of me was screaming, *"This is wrong! Get her out of here!"* And yet I kept going. Not listening to my gut, to my head or to my heart. I no longer knew what else to do.

From that moment on, Gabby was locked in. She was held in a secure centre, isolated from the world, away from her family and friends, away from me.

> She was not allowed outside to breathe fresh air and was shadowed by a nurse at all times.

> She was supervised while she was eating, and when she went to the toilet she had someone with her.

> For the remaining hours of the day and night, all she could do was sit in the isolated ward… doing art to keep herself occupied while she waited and … waited.

> She was asked every day, over and over again:

> "What do you think of the size of your bottom?"

> "Do you think about killing yourself?"

> "You should be angry, why aren't you angry?"

While I was allowed to visit, I wasn't allowed to bring her brothers and sisters for those first weeks. Gabby was allowed no other external visitors or contact except me. They tried for seven long weeks to get her to take antipsychotic medication. I had made it clear, over and over again, that she was not to be given that kind of medication, ever! Yet, every day when I wasn't there, they would harass Gabby and insist she take the medication.

She never did. She was incredibly brave and strong to stand up to them.

Gabby desperately sick and unhappy while big brother Kieran tries to comfort her

It was around this time that our family was becoming a blended family. I was totally supported and loved by my partner Shane (now husband). His strength was invaluable.

I'd work every day in a demanding job to pay the bills, then drive forty minutes to Logan to spend time with Gabby at night. Every visit tore at my heart. Gabby's spirit and the light in her eyes lessened each day. Little by little they were breaking her.

The ward was filled with violent and mentally ill teenagers, many with eating disorders. There was one young man who broke a glass door in the ward with a chair and ran away, only to be brought back by the police, and then ominously threaten Gabby later with a knife.

I knew I had to do everything I could to get Gabby out, but my dilemma was I still had no answers for her health. Gabby was still spontaneously vomiting everything she ate or drank.

CHAPTER 1: A MOTHER'S STORY

I set about doing everything I could to make our home safe for Gabby's return, including making arrangements for daily blood tests with our local doctor. We organised for older friends and siblings who were at university to tutor her as soon as she came home, so she could catch up on her schooling.

I rang the head psychiatrist at the hospital and told her that, once Gabby's potassium was levelled, we would take her home and care for her there. Within two hours of this phone conversation, the psychiatrist called me and advised she had put Gabby under an ITO – Involuntary Treatment Order. My heart sank with dread. I had no idea what this meant, but I knew something was very wrong.

The psychiatrist explained, "An ITO means you no longer have any say in Gabby's health, wellbeing or her treatments. Gabby will now stay at Logan for a minimum of another six weeks under our care and our treatment."

The psychiatrist went on to explain that it was in Gabby's best interests. After six weeks, I'd be given the chance to address this legal order by facing a Mental Health Tribunal.

This was wrong! This was ridiculous! This was unfounded!

The more I discovered, the more I realised that in the state of Queensland, the Mental Health Act allows this to be done, without any cause or explanation.

I fought this with every bone in my body.

At work, I negotiated a day off each week so I could focus on fighting this legally, to give Gabby freedom of choice back. All the while, the doctors were doing nothing to find a solution for her issues. She was stuck in the system and no matter where I looked, no-one cared, no-one offered help. They now had full reign to treat her only as a mental health patient, no longer having to listen to me as her advocate, insisting that they keep exploring other options.

During this, I was, as I had always been doing, searching for a diagnosis, an explanation for what was really wrong with Gabby's body. Desperately I contacted politicians, lawyers, other health professionals and allied health practitioners.

Researching online sources had become an obsession. I was searching daily for all possible causes, complications and treatments, but nothing of any substance ever explained what was happening to Gabby until…

That one moment, I will never forget it, I found the explanation.

The truth shall set her free

That particular day, I happened to search something using a different phrase, somehow some combination of words came to me and I clicked enter on the search. There it was!

> A hospital in the United States…
>
> the Nationwide Children's Organisation…
>
> had identified a syndrome.

As I read on, everything made sense. Gabby had been experiencing EVERY symptom. Everything they said about this syndrome matched her condition. It was as though an elusive puzzle piece, that I'd been desperately searching for years to find, had been placed into my hand… and the entire picture finally came together.

This had to be it… I was buzzing! Adrenaline coursed through my veins. My heart beat faster, my mouth was dry. I was excited and yet terrified at the same time.

All I could think was, *"Is this really it? Was it real or another red herring?"* Questions flooded into my mind, *"Why hadn't I found this earlier?"*

I continued through the night, checking and researching, looking for any clue. I ran to my partner and woke him. "This is it" I said, "I just know it!"

I contacted the hospital in the United States and was prepared to do anything to get her there. Raise money, ask, plead and beg for the funds. Whatever it took, I was going to do it.

It was going to cost approximately $250,000 but I was determined we could finally resolve this terrible situation for Gabby.

Then the miracle happened.

The specialists in America said, "There's also a specialist in Australia, who just happens to work out of a Children's Hospital in Brisbane, where you live. She's the only one in Australia who has trained with us."

I couldn't believe everyone had missed it, including me! Now there was ONE specialist in Australia trained to treat this rare condition, and she was here in the city, where we lived. At last! After years of suffering and trauma, humiliation for Gabby and fear of losing my daughter, the real journey could begin, with people who knew what was wrong and could do something about it.

I fought the Mental Health Panel to get Gabby released from the Mental Health ward at Logan. She was referred to the Australian specialist, Dr Frances Connor, who promptly took Gabby into her care. After, she was hospitalised and tested properly, we received a positive diagnosis.

Gabby had Rumination Syndrome.

At last, the right treatment could begin!

Over the following years, Gabby endured multiple operations that gave her access to adequate nutrition. However, treatment for this diagnosis was poorly funded by our medical system and private health. Attempts to overcome the cause and ongoing symptoms weren't available. Gabby now had a Mic-Key button and GJ tube in her belly so that she could have nutrition pumped into her body during the night. That way nutrients would stay in her body. It was required for her to have a specialised lower intestinal 48cm tubing with wire springs inserted to bypass the stomach, to make sure the regurgitating was avoided. Sometimes Gabby was able to be at home, but often she'd have to be then readmitted for all kinds of reasons, whether it was upgrading the tubes or other treatments.

On the beach-first time showing her life saving Mic-key GJ Tube

But at least the disease itself was finally being treated, as opposed to the band-aid solution of potassium infusions and having to endure the accusations and recrimination from medical and mental health teams who were treating the wrong condition and draining my daughter's will to survive.

Gabby was officially diagnosed, but in Australia there is very little experience with this functional gastrointestinal disorder. Sadly, our country's medical resources saw the lack of clinical trials for the treatments here in Australia as reason not to provide Gabby with the proven protocol that had a very high success rate in the US.

CHAPTER 1: A MOTHER'S STORY

Finally, after many meetings, and commitment by Gabby's specialist Dr Frances Connor, at the age of 18, Gabby was the first person in Australia with this diagnosis to undergo the rumination syndrome protocol at Queensland Children's Hospital.

The treatment was successful and on day one, the feeding tube was taken out. No more nightly feeds! Now it was time for Gabby to slowly retrain her stomach to digest food and the frequency of the vomiting would reduce over time.

I have the copy of the full letter that Dr Frances Connor shared with me after Gabby's recovery, but for now I wanted to show evidence of how lacking in awareness was; even in the medical fraternity of rumination syndrome. I have provided an excerpt below taken from her letter and in chapter 9, 'A Good Enough Mother,' you'll see the full letter from Dr Francis Connor of Gabby's recovery.

"Throughout this process, Gabrielle has shown incredible grit, determination and stoicism. She continued with her education and even with her martial arts (for which she has represented Australia previously). She continued to compete in and win martial arts competitions while unwell. Since being cured, she has resumed normal life with gusto, working hard both to earn a living also to catch up on lost educational opportunities. She is an incredibly high achieving, hard-working, down to earth and resilient young woman. Physically, she is extremely tough, having thrived despite her previous illness.

In summary, Gabrielle's eating disorder diagnosis was a misdiagnosis, reflecting a lack of awareness of her condition among many medical practitioners. She had a condition called rumination syndrome, which was cured years ago and is not likely to recur. During her previous health problems and subsequently, she has displayed extraordinary talent for getting on with the job, remaining positive and pushing herself to be the best she can be. She has been tested and been found to be an exceptional young person."

After thirteen days, Gabby was home and moving forward with her life.

> *I always knew in my heart that it wasn't a psychological disorder but a physical ailment. No doctor, specialist, paediatrician or nursing staff ever listened to, or believed me.*

If only I'd been able to over-ride their doubt and insist my intuition was right earlier. I wouldn't have been left to deal with such a huge secondary challenge.

My daughter was recovering which was so joyous for all of us to witness but now my secondary challenge was my personal Guilt with a capital 'G'.

I agonised over the fact that my daughter had been trapped within a mental institution to endure psychological torment and accusations and made to feel guilty for symptoms that were out of her control. I was distraught that Gabby's rights and freedom had been stolen and that she'd been treated without compassion for an incorrect and unfounded diagnosis of an eating disorder

> *All my daughter wanted was to be a normal kid, to be healthy and do her best at karate.*

The misdiagnosis of Gabby nearly killed her, and my mother's guilt nearly killed me.

I had to learn how to let go of this guilt for the sake of my sanity and for the benefit of my family. In Chapter 2 we'll dive into my 7 Step Formula to let go of guilt, but first we'll delve into the mistakes we all make from time to time.

The difference between shame and guilt is the difference betweewn 'I am bad' and 'I did something bad'

Dr Brene Brown

CHAPTER 2
Let Go of Guilt –
the Mistakes We Make as Parents

A Mother's Guilt

Most often a mothers' guilt is not due to life threatening challenges like the ones our family experienced. Often, it's about whether the decisions we do or don't make are right or wrong:

- not knowing whether you chose the 'right' school
- not understanding why your child is left out at school
- doubting you did the right thing about x or y
- perhaps there was a time when you had a 'feeling' but you didn't listen to that inner voice until it was too late

Here's the thing I've learned about a mothers' guilt, sometimes we doubt this 'feeling' because we can't verbalise what we feel. This chapter will help you gain clarity around your feelings and help you get on with being a guilt-free, loving mother.

Life can get in the way. How to let go of the guilt.

It was a gorgeous Saturday at home, and I had household chores to complete. The children were playing inside for a little while as I

CHAPTER 2: LET GO OF GUILT – THE MISTAKES WE MAKE AS PARENTS

cleaned the house. My little boy, Kieran, was stretching the limits, as six-year old's love to do. He was jumping over the back of the lounge and landing just near one of my prized Mediterranean style concrete pedestals. (Believe me when I say it was the look then.)

After several warnings that I'd send him to his room if he didn't stop, there was an almighty scream. Kieran had landed on the ground and his arm had smashed against the pedestal. I ran to pick him up, there were tears, and there were cuddles amid my 'I told you so's'.

Kieran sucked back the tears and asked to go to bed to have a lie down. The next day at gymnastics, I noticed a grimace on his face whenever he had to move his arm. After a trip to the family doctor, I was told that he had a broken wrist!

As the plaster was carefully applied, I could feel the guilt slowly rising. My poor little boy had been so brave, I couldn't apologise enough. We laugh about it now, but at the time my guilt screamed at me, "You really should have listened to him, he was only doing what came naturally. He was playing, and he hurt himself."

I had ignored it.

Kieran

That 'feeling' stayed with me for years, even though he was fine and loved having a cast to brag to his friends, my mother's guilt niggled in the back of my mind. A sinking feeling lodged into the place in my body where guilty feelings skulk. Time and time again, my thoughts came back to haunt me, "You should have, could have…"

Just like the guilt I felt later with Gabby, I knew it was interfering with my love for my children. Whenever I had loving thoughts toward them, that little voice would echo, "Yes, but…" Then that sinking feeling would start up and the guilt would swallow up the love. To me, it felt as though love could no longer feel pure, it was always tinged with guilt. I knew I had to do something to eliminate the guilt and open back up to my children again.

Layers of guilt

When Gabby was hospitalised, there were many things I felt guilty about. My mind would become saturated with questions that, if I let them, would lead down the dark path that ended with me thinking, "It's my fault, I'm not good enough." My thoughts would race:

- Was it me? Was I contributing to her health challenge?
- The stress of the divorce must be causing this extreme issue for her.
- The divorce was my choice, what other choices had I made that had influenced Gabby's health?
- Did my tension, fear and/or anxiety show when I spoke with the doctors and nurses? Was I keeping myself calm enough to achieve what was important for her without alienating them and becoming 'that mother'?

I have to say, sometimes I really was 'that mother', but I had to be just to get someone to listen to us and investigate further.

I'd been so worried when her potassium dropped – I wondered was there anything else I should be doing to keep those levels up? I was put on this earth to keep my children healthy and strong, to see them through to adulthood, and there were so many times I felt I just wasn't cutting it.

I remember one time in particular, after Gabby had already received the correct diagnosis, being called in to the hospital for a meeting. Gabby's usual specialist was away so this particular

CHAPTER 2: LET GO OF GUILT – THE MISTAKES WE MAKE AS PARENTS

doctor knew the situation, but wasn't as familiar with our background. He repeatedly referred to the *psychological* issues of Gabby's syndrome.

I politely corrected him by reminding him that rumination syndrome is a physical ailment, and to please stop referring to Gabby as though she had a psychological disorder.

He didn't listen and continued to refer to the psychological even though I continued to correct him. Well, I lost it.

I was very loud and demonstrative and stormed out of the room in tears. I had a tantrum. Of course, this was a mistake. I was not proud of my conduct and was certainly not contributing to working towards the best outcome by behaving like this. I eventually re-entered the room with my tail between my legs.

The *Specialist* apologised.

I apologised as well and the meeting came to an end without a satisfactory resolution. It was not one of my proudest moments. This was yet another thing I felt I had failed to manage well for Gabby.

Still to this day, I check in and worry if I'm meeting my adult children and stepchildren's needs. Am I doing the best that I can for them? As a mother I'm sure you agree, it doesn't matter how old they are, we will always want the best for them and hope we can provide that for them.

Exercise - We all make mistakes

In the first column of the chart below make a list of times in your life when you've made mistakes. Examples of things you used to, or still, hold guilt about. In the second column, list the 'inner critic' thoughts you tell yourself about this (then and now). I've given examples of personal experiences of mine to help you understand the process.

Mistake	Inner critic guilt voice
I forgot to pick the kids up from school. A teacher rang to say they were the last kids playing and everyone was waiting to close the school for the day. I'd been immersed in work, and time had vanished. Now, if it was today, I would have set an alarm on my phone, but back then we didn't have phones with alarms.	• How can you forget your kids? • What if something had happened? • You're a bad mother • What must the teacher think? • You're making work more important than them • They'll feel like they aren't important to me • I can't believe I could do that to my kids
After her tooth fell out, Gabby woke to look in the glass to see the coin that the tooth fairy had left while she slept. But her tooth was still there. I had forgotten to swap it. I distracted her for 10 minutes, and when she returned, the 'tooth fairy' had miraculously replaced the tooth with a $5 note (the only money in my purse). Unwittingly, I'd set a precedent. Each of my child's eyes glinted with expectation because now they knew they'd each get $5 per tooth.	• Stupid me for forgetting • It's my fault, now I'm stuck with this • Why didn't I do it last night? • All I needed to do was go in to her room before I went to bed, so stupid!!! • I ruined this gorgeous magical moment and made it all about the money!

Some of those examples, on reflection, have turned out to be quite funny, and some of the examples of mistakes I've mentioned in the book so far were more serious. But we're human, and mistakes help us learn. (Once we let go of the guilt that is.) When we learn, we grow, evolve and become better human beings, better role models, better mothers.

Now it's your turn. Make a list of five mistakes you criticise yourself for. Write down a couple of lighter mistakes, and a couple of more serious ones. BE BRAVE, remember nothing changes if you don't learn from mistakes.

Once you make your list, I'll help you let go of the guilt with my 7 Step Formula.

Mistake	**Inner critic guilt voice**

Burnt bacon for breakfast

When my children were quite young, I read somewhere that protein helps us focus. It especially helps children who find it hard to stay still in class. So, I resolved to provide bacon and eggs for breakfast each morning for my kids. Protein for breakfast would especially help my very active children, Ebony being a classical ballerina and very physically active, Gabby being the karate kid and athletic star and Kieran for his mental focus during studies and his karate training also and Sarah for her dedication to her academics.

> *As a working mum, I must have had my super mum cape on when I made this decision, (and we all know that those capes can get a few holes in them from time to time).*

Now, I can be known to bite off more than I can chew if I feel it's important, and so my commitment to follow through on my decision began.

Each morning I would race down to the kitchen with good intentions. I'd place the bacon on the grill, race back upstairs, check that all the kids were up and getting ready for the day. I'd race back and forth between their rooms and mine, get myself dressed and ready for work, then rush back downstairs just ahead of the smoke alarm shrilling through the house from the kitchen.

No matter how organised I tried to be, every morning we had a house filled with 'smoking bacon.' Some of the bacon pieces were burnt, some, if we were lucky, were nice and crispy. I would then toss eggs in the pan and breakfast was served to groans from the children, "You've burnt the bacon again, mum!"

I'd give a loosely intentioned apology (perhaps I wasn't that sorry, as I was doing the best I could with the time I had). I had high expectations of myself as a mother and did what I could to meet

CHAPTER 2: LET GO OF GUILT – THE MISTAKES WE MAKE AS PARENTS

everyone's needs and my standards. Morning after morning my beautiful children would crunch their way through the protein because I thought I was doing the best for them.

As they got older, and then stepchildren arrived to expand our wonderful family, I would, at times, forget the school and after school pickup or drop off arrangements. Was I meant to be at the school or the train station, or at an after-school sporting practice? Who knew sometimes? That was before the days of all children having a mobile phone, so sometimes one or more of the kids would arrive home or at my work, sweating and a little exasperated.

Gabby, Sarah, Ebony, Kieran, sharp minds and energetic

We're all human beings, we're all trying to juggle life, work and play. I remember frequently reminding myself, as long as they're safe, I haven't neglected them or put them in harm's way, it's okay to make mistakes.

It's okay to let go of perfection as a parent, the perfect parent doesn't exist.

The perfect parent is you, doing the best that you can with the skills, knowledge and resources that you have. You are perfect for your child. It's time to let go of that guilt with the help of my 7 Step Formula.

7 Step Formula to let go of guilt and trust your parenting skill

Step 1: **Curious**	When triggered by guilt or other disruptive emotions, get curious. If the emotion is super challenging, start by blinking three times and roll your eyes in a slow circle clockwise then anti-clockwise. (This is a concept my mentor, Maggie Wilde taught me, and it works to diffuse the intensity of a reaction.) You'll be able to think more clearly and become curious about your reaction and whatever or whoever triggered you to react. Curiosity gives you the power to change your reaction.
Step 2: **Where?**	Curiosity has now helped you find a little space between you and the guilt or other emotion. Notice the position of your reaction? Is it somewhere specific in your body, perhaps a feeling or thought in your head, or is it outside of you?
Step 3: **What?**	What is your reaction? Is it a thought, emotion or sensation? If you can't name it at first, be okay to say 'blank'. Then roll your eyes and blink, take a deep breath and try to name it again.
Step 4: **Half**	Observe the reaction using the breathing and eye roll cycle until the intensity of the thought, sensation or emotion is about half of where it started. (If it stays the same, that's okay too. Do three cycles and move on to Step 5.)
Step 5: **Purpose**	Ask the reaction: If it had a positive purpose, what would that purpose be? If the purpose is a negative purpose at first, keep asking what is the positive purpose? It doesn't make it right, it's just a purpose.
Step 6: **Brave**	Be brave, give the reaction a voice. Don't ignore it or hide from it anymore. You can't change what you don't face. As my mentor recommends: Ask silently in your mind, "If the thought, emotion or sensation had a voice, what might it say?"

CHAPTER 2: LET GO OF GUILT – THE MISTAKES WE MAKE AS PARENTS

Step 7: **Gratitude**	Be grateful that you understand more clearly now. If you can't find gratitude as yet, repeat the 7 Steps. For strong reactions, we may need to do the steps two or more times.

Measure the intensity of the original reaction on a scale of 0-10 again (with 10 being the worst.)

If your reaction is still above a 3 on the scale, repeat the 7 steps until the reaction feels clear

Keep practicing the steps to let go of guilt. It will get easier the more you use the formula. Come back to this chapter at any time to address guilt when it arises. The thing about guilt is, it will pop up many, many times in your life as a parent. See each time it does as a chance to get better at loving your child guilt-free.

Reflections

I've asked my wonderful children to write their reflections for this book. I promised them that they were safe to say whatever they wished, to give a true perception on any topic they felt was important to them. Confronting for me? Absolutely. But that's what this book is all about. Being vulnerable, and to share so that we can all learn.

Here are the reflections from one of the nicest young men I've had the privilege to know, my eldest son Kieran. He has a kind heart, is handsome and loving. He is such a good person and I especially love that we have shared many hours debating life!

Kieran's reflections

My beautiful Kieran

For me it's always been a bit difficult being the odd one out in the family. The only boy, the only one interested in technology, the only heavy reader. I was always…different. That's not to say I didn't love being a member of my family. I certainly have more joyous memories than I can count. But there was always a through-line of "difference". In spite of this, or perhaps because of it, I have a strong, deep relationship with my family.

My sisters and I would fight a lot as children, as teenagers, and even into adulthood. We would also spend a large amount of time just hanging out, being friends with each other. To this day any one of us would do anything to help out each other.

Mum and I clashed often, especially through my teenage years. Often over simply going to sleep, as I would read through the night. Some fights continued simply due to stubbornness. However, Mum would always go out of her way to ensure I was able to do what I needed to do, and able to live as stress-free as possible.

Over the years we have learned one another's boundaries and grown to understand each other. Today I am happy to say I could not have asked for a better mother to raise me, through the good, the hard and the absolutely messed up times. My family is definitely one of the best.

In the next chapter I've tackled the topic of perfectionism and expectations. Once I learned how to manage my own expectations of what a 'good' mother should be and accept that I sometimes couldn't meet the expectations of others, myself and even my children, then mother's guilt subsided. When I was able to accept that I was doing the best that I could, it gave me a renewed energy in life.

It was easier to know it than to explain why I know it.

Sherlock Holmes

CHAPTER 3
Near Enough Has to Be Good Enough

Letting go of perfect parenting.

In the last chapter I referred to that super mum cape we try to wear. You know; the super mum cape that exemplifies we are master of all, nurse, mother, educator, fit and healthy, funny, taxi driver, best friend, good daughter (yes we often carry expectations that we try to meet about being somebody's child too), a sexy partner, and every other persona imaginable.

Well, the super mum cape is wonderful in theory, however that expectation sets us up to add to the bucket of guilt we already carry. Mums, the cape is a pathway to feeling like a failure.

Of course, we cannot be perfect, no-one really is (even that perfect looking mum at the school drop off, who is coiffed to perfection, slim, dressed divinely, and with skin glowing with health), even she has bad days.

> *Doing our absolute best with what we know and have now, simply MUST be enough.*

If we do our best on the day and don't quite cut it, and we embrace letting go of the guilt about it, then we can learn from this and get to try again tomorrow. Isn't that what we are trying to teach our children? Perfection isn't possible, but learning, growing and doing our best is always the best way.

Do we want to lead by example and show vulnerability to our children, so that they understand and model themselves as balanced human beings, prepared to make mistakes and have compassion and understanding for themselves and others? Or do we want our children to be anxious perfectionists who can't ever feel like they're good enough?

Forgiveness of yourself and acceptance that you are enough, these are your greatest opportunities as a mother to teach your child that near enough is better than not trying at all. That when they try their best, it is good enough. Then they have the opportunity to learn and go to the next level.

I remember the first Christmas we had after I separated from my first husband. I was a single mum and money was tight to say the least. Our family Christmas tradition was not unlike most families in the western world. There had been an abundance each year of gifts, food and love.

Well, this year there was an abundance of love but the other two were sadly lacking. I knew the children's dad was in a better financial position and could provide some lovely presents and festivities for them, so I suggested they could have Christmas Eve and Christmas Day with him to enjoy the abundance. I'd pick them up later in the afternoon to celebrate Christmas with them at home more frugally.

I was feeling guilty. I'd chosen to separate from the children's father, I was the one who'd created this shortage, so I went about trying to make the best of what we had. For gifts, I chose things

I already had that were significant to our family. I wrapped them and gave them with love to my children as I shared the story around the gift.

One of the gifts was a lovely silver bangle that my dad had given me for my 12th birthday (my dad passed before I had my children), so this was very special to me. As it turned out, along with the significance to me, it was special to my child.

That first 'frugal' Christmas created a new tradition for our family of playing board games and having fun. Creating a new tradition from something simple and yet so significant provided a memory of love and abundance that I'm proud of. It's a tradition we continued with our blended family. Our holidays together are full of fun, laughter and loving competitiveness. Near enough really was good enough.

When it's time to say no.

There were times when my young teenagers were invited to parties. I dreaded those invitations because I knew there would be alcohol. I knew I'd have to be strong and stand by my convictions as a mother.

I said no and was called a 'mean mum' by whichever teenager had asked. After a while, they just knew not to ask at all. Saying no was important to me as a mother because it was aligned with my values. I knew that keeping them safe and passing on standards and values that were for their welfare, were for their greater good. It was important for me to be a mum, not their best friend. Too often, some parents believe it's better to be their child's friend instead of the rule maker and disciplinarian. A child needs to have security, safety and guidelines to feel safe and develop into a strong, high-integrity adult. I believe it is our commitment and role as a mother to teach our children how to be an adult. They have plenty of friends and only one mother/stepmother. (More about the importance of this in Chapter 7.)

CHAPTER 3: NEAR ENOUGH HAS TO BE GOOD ENOUGH

Have you ever had to say no and maintain your conviction?

Saying no can be hard, it can be brutal with the repercussions of a disgruntled teenager. But for me, no matter how hard it felt, and no matter how harsh the teenager thought I was being, I stuck to my beliefs. The answer was always 'no'.

I believe that because of this consistency and these stringent guidelines in their early teens, where I was still responsible for their safety, I shaped the responsible, caring humans they have grown to be. They know now too, it was important for them to know the strength of no, when no was required.

When have you known it simply had to be no, even if it pained you? Did you feel guilty about it? Or do you have trouble saying no because you think you'll disappoint your children? Let's deal with that guilt now.

7 Step Formula to let go of guilt and trust your parenting skills

Step 1: **Curious**	When triggered by guilt or other disruptive emotions, get curious. If the emotion is super challenging, start by blinking three times and roll your eyes in a slow circle clockwise then anti-clockwise. (This is a concept my mentor, Maggie Wilde taught me and it works to diffuse the intensity of a reaction.) You'll be able to think more clearly and become curious about your reaction and whatever or whoever triggered you to react. Curiosity gives you the power to change your reaction.
Step 2: **Where?**	Curiosity has now helped you find a little space between you and the guilt or other emotion. Notice the position of your reaction? Is it somewhere specific in your body, perhaps a feeling or thought in your head, or is it outside of you?
Step 3: **What?**	What is your reaction? Is it a thought, emotion or sensation? If you can't name it at first, be okay to say 'blank'. Then roll your eyes and blink, take a deep breath and try to name it again.

Step 4: **Half**	Observe the reaction using the breathing and eye roll cycle until the intensity of the thought, sensation or emotion is about half of where it started. (If it stays the same, that's okay too. Do three cycles and move on to Step 5.)	
Step 5: **Purpose**	Ask the reaction: If it had a positive purpose, what would that purpose be? If the purpose is a negative purpose at first, keep asking what is the positive purpose? It doesn't make it right, it's just a purpose.	
Step 6: **Brave**	Be brave, give the reaction a voice. Don't ignore it or hide from it anymore. You can't change what you don't face. As my mentor recommends: Ask silently in your mind, "If the thought, emotion or sensation had a voice, what might it say?"	
Step 7: **Gratitude**	Be grateful that you understand more clearly now. If you can't find gratitude as yet, repeat the 7 Steps. For strong reactions, we may need to do the steps two or more times.	

Measure the intensity of the original reaction on a scale of 0-10 again (with 10 being the worst.)

If your reaction is still above a 3 on the scale, repeat the 7 steps until the reaction feels clear

Knowing when to say yes

At times, even when I saw so many impossible hurdles to overcome, if I had a belief that it was important to say yes, then I did. I trusted that we could work it out.

In the times of money shortage and frugality, one of my daughters competed in Canada for a Karate World Championship, and the other I accompanied to Italy where her ballet school performed for a week. After the performances we spent time together travelling through parts of Italy. No matter how hard it was financially at a very tough time as a single mum, I wanted each of them to have a special experience. At the time it seemed the funds were provided by the universe, but we did it, it just worked out.

CHAPTER 3: NEAR ENOUGH HAS TO BE GOOD ENOUGH

Sometimes, when you just know it's right, it's important to have the belief in yourself that you can just say yes.

Gabby's Karate Kata

Have you ever said yes, without knowing how you would achieve something?

Every new school year was an enormous drain on the finances, especially after Christmas and a family holiday. All of the children had either worn out or grown out of their sports shoes and their school shoes. I'd need to find money for eight new pairs of shoes, four sets of school books, often new school bags, and often new uniforms were needed too. Somehow, I did it, I don't know how. (All without robbing a bank!)

Ebony was a fully committed ballerina for most of her childhood and into adulthood. Those beautiful ballet pointes would wear out very fast. At one stage, she needed a new pair every three weeks. Then there were the new stockings, leotards, tutus, and costumes. I'd agonise sometimes over how to afford it all, but I just found a way.

Can you think of any times that have been that way for you? You just didn't have an option and you simply made it happen.

My children look back at those times with gratitude and amazement at what we achieved when things were so tight financially.

Near enough is good enough

As mothers we're all doing the best we can with what we have. The pressure to put on the super mum cape, grit our teeth and push through is enormous. But it's a pressure we put on ourselves. The truth is sometimes things will go right, other times they'll go wrong. Sometimes we can say yes, and sometimes we have to say no. And remember, there is no such thing as perfection, near enough is good enough.

Consider your latest mantras to be

"I do the best I can with the skills and resources I have right now."

"I forgive myself for not being able to be everything to everyone."

"I am open to the lessons my children teach me."

"I HAVE enough, I DO enough, I AM enough."

"I can do anything, but I can't do everything"

"I can, I will, I am".

Feel free to adapt this into your own language to make the mantras more powerful for you. Change it wherever you need to, make it your own. That's where the strength is.

CHAPTER 3: NEAR ENOUGH HAS TO BE GOOD ENOUGH

One of the greatest gifts your children can give you, is grandchildren. The strength and compassion, the great love for family and others, is abundantly apparent in the life of my eldest daughter Sarah. She is intelligent and wise and takes great care of all who she loves. Known even as a child by the neighbourhood kids as 'mum', Sarah invests great love and mothering to her exquisite children.

Sarah's reflections

My beautiful Sarah

Trying to think of the bad things my mum did when we were growing up, I had to really think hard. However, if you'd asked me when I was a child, I could have rattled off a few. It just goes to show that what may seem like a big deal at the time, really isn't. Things like the chore lists over school holidays or not letting me buy those hot chips while on holidays just before dinner time. Overall, mum seemed to know what she was doing, even if she didn't think so. As a child, and even more so now as a mum myself, I was in awe of how she managed to do it all; working, after school activities, home-cooked meals, holidays, birthdays and events. We always knew when it was a cleaning Saturday in our home. Mum would be up and moving around the house…very early…and then the music would start – Michael Bublé or Robbie Williams… we were always super tired those mornings. ☺

A challenge I hear repeatedly from mums in my clinic is that they have this deep inner yearning to want to fix everything for their children. That when there are things they can't fix, the guilt and anxiety this causes can be debilitating. I remember this feeling when Gabby was so ill. The sense of helplessness was tangible and kept me up most nights.

I wanted to address this topic in the following chapter, because it is one of the most frequent 'pains' I hear from mums no matter where they are in the world.

*I love you no matter
what you do!
I may not like it, we may
argue and disagree but,
I will always
Love you!*

CHAPTER 4
When I Can't Fix Everything

It's time to share with you something that has caused me great pain.

I'm choosing to be more vulnerable than I usually am, especially in a public forum, because I want my honesty to help you realise that it's okay to be you just as you are. I want to inspire you to know you're good enough, and in this way, provide peace and understanding for you as a mum too.

As you've already read, Gabby was very ill, for a very long time, without a diagnosis or any help from the medical world to give her back her life.

Even though we struggled, we tried to keep positive with the conviction that there was a solution, we just hadn't found it yet. But life was overwhelming.

I was going through a relentlessly difficult divorce and trying to provide and support all my children while in a job that was barely paying bills. At the same time, I was also searching for ways to heal my daughter.

And then, the system took her away, essentially accusing me of not doing enough, or conversely doing something to cause her 'psychological disorder'. In their eyes I was a parent who was at fault.

Over the time since, I've worked therapeutically to move past the trauma and pain and really thought I'd achieved this. After Gabby became well, I did my best to deal with the guilt and move on.

But deep down, I knew there was something still niggling at me.

I wasn't entirely able to heal those years of trauma. There was a kind of pressure in my body whenever I thought about leaving my daughter at the high-security mental ward. It was like a massive lump in the front of my throat, almost choking me. My body was still reacting.

The layers of guilt

It wasn't until many years after, as I began writing this book, that I was able to get to the root of the problem. I was away on a writer's retreat with my mentor and publisher, Maggie Wilde. We were working through the steps of the 7 Step Formula, testing it out on different aspects of mother's guilt to ensure it was adaptable for all different circumstances.

Was it easy? Yes, the steps were easy, but was facing what was there and the emotions that were still lingering all those years later easy? No, that wasn't easy at all.

We worked through the steps many times and each time another layer of pain, guilt, fear or shame showed up. As we continued to clear the old emotion, the energy and the sensation of the emotion would shift to another space in my body. It was like peeling an onion, we would clear one emotion and my body would lead me somewhere else.

It was apparent that my body had a voice, unsaid words, fears and hopes, trapped over these many years.

Within 10 minutes, I came to a realisation, an awareness and complete healing that released the guilt of years of trauma.

I realised that Gabby being locked in that high-security mental ward was actually a gift. I needed that space and time to get in touch with my creative mind in order to access the answer as to how to find her cure.

More specifically than that, to help my daughter heal.

> *Gabby got better because I had space in my head, to think of ways I hadn't thought of before.*

For years, the guilt, worry, and fear had busied my mind. Every waking moment was filled with the knowing that Gabby's diagnosis had been wrong, that she did indeed have a physical illness, not a psychological one as the doctors wanted us to believe. I knew this to be true with every cell of my being, yet the conflict and stress existed because I couldn't find what that illness was.

If it was psychological, then why wasn't what they were doing after years of treatment helping her. Why was she on her death bed? The overwhelm and conflict that filled my mind had shut my creativity off so that my intuition was only 'this feeling'. I had no space in my head to hear my intuition and find the path to find Rumination Disorder.

> *The longer I worried and busied myself with how to fix Gabby, the longer it took me to find the solution. I'd been exhausted but determined, and there was no room to breathe.*

> *When Gabby was locked away in the psychological ward, there was finally room for the solution to come to me.*

CHAPTER 4: WHEN I CAN'T FIX EVERYTHING

Do you have something that has lingered on? Perhaps something you are dealing with right now?

Let's go through the exact steps I've been using for years, the steps I used with my mentor to finally find peace about the guilt of leaving my daughter in that place. If I can do it, you can too. Be brave, I know you can do this. Let's find the space in your head heart by releasing past guilt.

Think of something now, rate it on intensity on a scale of 0-10, 10 being the most.

7 Step Formula to let go of guilt and trust your parenting skills: Simplicity

Step 1: **Curious**	When triggered by guilt or other disruptive emotions, get curious. If the emotion is super challenging, start by blinking three times and roll your eyes in a slow circle clockwise then anti-clockwise. (This is a concept my mentor, Maggie Wilde taught me and it works to diffuse the intensity of a reaction.) You'll be able to think more clearly and become curious about your reaction and whatever or whoever triggered you to react. Curiosity gives you the power to change your reaction.
Step 2: **Where?**	Curiosity has now helped you find a little space between you and the guilt or other emotion. Notice the position of your reaction? Is it somewhere specific in your body, perhaps a feeling or thought in your head, or is it outside of you?
Step 3: **What?**	What is your reaction? Is it a thought, emotion or sensation? If you can't name it at first, be okay to say 'blank'. Then roll your eyes and blink, take a deep breath and try to name it again.
Step 4: **Half**	Observe the reaction using the breathing and eye roll cycle until the intensity of the thought, sensation or emotion is about half of where it started. (if it stays the same, that's okay too. Do three cycles and move on to Step 5.)

Step 5: **Purpose**	Ask the reaction: If it had a positive purpose, what would that purpose be? If the purpose is a negative purpose at first, keep asking what is the positive purpose? It doesn't make it right, it's just a purpose.
Step 6: **Brave**	Be brave, give the reaction a voice. Don't ignore it or hide from it anymore. You can't change what you don't face. As my mentor recommends: Ask silently in your mind, "If the thought, emotion or sensation had a voice, what might it say?"
Step 7: **Gratitude**	Be grateful that you understand more clearly now. If you can't find gratitude as yet, repeat the 7 Steps. For strong reactions, we may need to do the steps two or more times.

Measure the intensity of the original reaction on a scale of 0-10 again (with 10 being the worst.)

If your reaction is still above a 3 on the scale, repeat the 7 steps until the reaction feels clear

And sometimes, you know what? You just don't get it right. Try as you may to be the best parent you can, no matter how perfect you try to be, sometimes you just don't get it right.

Sarah's story

One of my children, Sarah, complained repeatedly about a sore throat. Doctors couldn't find the cause. She was hospitalised at the end of every term over several years, in dreadful pain and with no explanation. I'd tell her to eat something, have a piece of toast or fruit. She would cry and say it hurt too much.

Five years later, after checking with countless doctors and allied health professionals, she was diagnosed with a severe case of peritonsillar abscess, also known as quinsy — an abscess hiding behind the tonsils. The ENT surgeon rushed her into theatre.

My poor darling was telling me, and I just didn't know. I couldn't fix what I didn't know. Sometimes you just cannot fix something until you know what needs to be fixed.

What's my definition of madness?

Holding onto guilt when you don't know yet what you need to know to fix something. Even doctors are only human, and humans can get it wrong. Mums are human too, and we get it wrong sometimes.

> You can follow along with Lynne doing the 7 Step Formula by accessing a complimentary video here
> www.agoodenoughmother.com/resources

Sometimes, no matter what we try to do as a mum, when big life changes happen that effect one member or all of the family, life can get a little scary for everyone too. Unexpected change, and even expected ones, can trigger all kinds of reactions from you and your children. In Chapter 5, I address the effects of change on the family and how to make the transition a little easier.

*Family
like branches on a tree
we all grow in
different directions,
but our roots remain
as one.*

CHAPTER 5
When Change Happens

Change is normal, it's natural, and it's inevitable.

It's when you feel the change is out of your control that the effects can be dramatic.

There are two basic types of change - the changes we choose, and the forced changes.

Our children go through many stages — baby, toddler, tweenager, teenager, and young adult. These changes are normal and natural, even if they're hard to deal with sometimes. Parents witness the changes their children go through and children also witness the changes their parents go through, both forced and/or chosen.

Moving House

When the children were young, especially before the Brady Bunch years, we moved to a new house many times - about 12 times in 20years including three interstate moves. Some may feel this number seems excessive, however each move happened for good reasons.

Interstate move, new home, new school

Along with the usual mayhem of kid stuff, food, nappies, finding new schools, new doctors, hairdressers, friends etc, we pretty much learnt how to move efficiently and as a team. A few of the essential rules to make these transitions work well, were:

Essential rules

1. Each child was in charge of their own room with some help from siblings and me, to sort, discard, pack and then unpack in the new home. This gave them ownership and a sense of achievement.

2. It was a priority that the new house would be looking and feeling like home within the first week, so the disruption to everyone's lives was minimised.

3. I turned the move into an adventure…how exciting, we're going to be able to be closer to school, your friends, the park. All the things that were important to the children at the time.

Divorce

For a parent, divorce can be either a chosen or a forced change. You're either the one choosing the circumstance, or you become the one who's at the effect of it.

For our children however, divorce is always a forced change. Often no matter what their parent's relationship is like, kids don't want their parents to separate, they are not naturally prepared for that forced change to happen. When it does, we not only need to adjust for the change we experience but adapt our communication and actions for the change our children will experience too.

Divorce happens. Sadly, divorce rates worldwide are between 40-50%. Divorce rates for couples with children is as much as 40% lower than those without children.

We are here to talk about coping with change, and with the percentages so high, it's inevitable that there needs to be some understanding and strategies available. Believe it or not, very few people get married with the plan to divorce. For now, let's talk about the majority.

Three steps to protect your children from what they don't need to see.

You need some form of support — a professional or a friend, who just listens to you. If that's not available here's an option. Make sure the kids are safe, drive around the corner out of sight, pull over with the radio blaring, and think, cry, or move. Give yourself permission to let it out.

> *I gave myself permission to cry, but not in the presence of my children.*

If one or both parties are angry with each other, or when the relationship is a bit rocky and things are simply too volatile, or when every cell of your body is screaming that you want to be heard, just pause and ask yourself, "Is this the thing that's right for the kids to hear right now? Do they really need to know this?" If not, then try these three steps.

1. If you can, step away and breathe. If you can't step away, silently step away within and breathe.

   Learn how to Take a Breath with Lynne at www.agoodenoughmother.com/resources

2. Ask yourself, is this really what the kids need to hear now?

3. Work through the 7 Step Formula.

These steps give you something to interrupt the energy. They're also a great strategy when the kids are getting a bit out of control, having tantrums or acting out.

Always with divorce or family trauma, check in with your kids, and where it's possible and calm, have both parents present. Children are often more capable of understanding the world around them than they are given credit for, especially regarding emotions. Ask, "Are you coping? Can you think of a better way that we could be behaving?" All age appropriate of course, but as a mother, trust your intuition as to what's right and most helpful for your child.

I'm sure there have been times when, like me, you've wished you hadn't said things. Look back in hindsight and ask yourself, what might you have done differently? Or perhaps, if it was your best friend and you were giving them advice, what would you say to them to help?

When communication gets out of hand in these unfortunate circumstances, what do you tell your child about divorce or separation?

Timing is everything.

1. Only talk about it when you are absolutely certain it's happening.

2. Spare your children the details but answer their questions.

3. Tell your children with both parents present, don't play the blame game and then observe for unusual behaviour and reactions.

4. Keep the conversation going, check in often and make sure they're feeling understood.

5. Talk about feelings, and let your children make some decisions about how it's going to play out.

Changing schools

For some children, changing schools can be the worst thing in the world.

Ebony was dancing from the young age of three and was passionate about it, but she also loved netball and was involved in school, club and rep teams. When she was 12 years old, her ballet teacher told her that she would have to choose – ballet or netball. Ebony thought long and hard on this and we discussed it extensively. I made it clear that it was ultimately her decision. I trusted her to come to a decision that was best for her. It may sound like a lot of pressure for a 12-year-old, but she was a mature, sensible young lady, and I knew, as her mother, what she was capable of. She chose ballet and she's never regretted this decision.

With her choice in mind, I encouraged her to consider a different dance school that taught the more accepted curriculum of RAD instead of the Bolshoi she was studying. It took her 12 months to come to terms with this, as the change was riddled with feelings of guilt because of her sense of loyalty to her teacher. Eventually she changed dance schools, and, after catching up with the other students, excelled and found that opportunities opened up for her. Yes, change was difficult, but when we follow our heart it can open up to so much more.

Ebony on stage

Consider how much choice you have given your children and what you take into consideration for how much say they actually have. Taking in age appropriateness and trusting your intuition is vital, as is encouraging your child (no matter what age) to trust their intuition also.

CHAPTER 5: WHEN CHANGE HAPPENS

I may have mentioned before that Gabby was a huge tomboy. At the age of five, she demanded her beautiful curly, thick mane be cut off, so she'd be just like her brother! She took her earrings out and began dressing in boys' clothes to be more comfortable for playing soccer, climbing, running and doing what she loved (NEVER playing with dolls ☺).

Her old school allowed shorts and she felt comfortable in the uniform. However, her new school didn't. She worked out that she'd have to wear a dress, and so decided to fit in she'd have to grow her hair. Yes, children know and trust their intuition so much better than adults at times. She had an innate knowing that she'd need to be able to re-invent herself so she could assimilate more easily. This made the change so much easier for her, and she also found she was happy with her decision and the new school.

When change is hard

This isn't to say that when change was required, it was easy. The kids did worry about it, so much so, that whenever we were moving to a new house, or there was major change in their lives, Kieran would come down with croup. No matter what I did to reassure him, or take into account his feelings, it would always happen. Poor little guy, in the middle of summer, new house, new school, whatever it was, and he'd be struggling to breathe.

A wonderful strategy that I use in clinic now, as I work with children for all sorts of worries, change and even issues with bullying, is this marvellous process, based on a protocol called the Rewind Technique developed by a UK clinical hypnotherapist, Mark Tyrrell.

Rewind Technique

1. Sit with your child with a big drawing pad and colours – crayons, pencils or watercolour.

2. Ask them to draw what they are worried about. It may be the monster under the bed, it may be the kid at school that was mean, it may just be something around the fear of change in a situation.

3. Now, the fun begins. Take it in turns adding something funny. If it's a person, perhaps add fairy wings, a rabbits' fluffy tail, rainbow stockings, big long clown shoes, perhaps glittery ballet pumps. Or maybe make each person in the drawing a different animal – add a long giraffe neck, cat ears, crocodile bulgy eyes. You get the idea – have fun!

4. Give the characters a funny voice, e.g. Donald Duck, Alvin the Chipmunk, tiny, tiny ant voice.

5. When the child is giggling and happy with the completed artwork, you may tell a funny story, or ask the child to tell you the funny story about the drawing.

This simply dilutes and releases the fear.

CHAPTER 5: WHEN CHANGE HAPPENS

7 Step Formula to let go of guilt and trust your parenting skills: Fear of change

Step 1: **Curious**	When triggered by guilt or other disruptive emotions, get curious. If the emotion is super challenging, start by blinking three times and roll your eyes in a slow circle clockwise then anti-clockwise. (This is a concept my mentor, Maggie Wilde taught me and it works to diffuse the intensity of a reaction.) You'll be able to think more clearly and become curious about your reaction and whatever or whoever triggered you to react. Curiosity gives you the power to change your reaction.	
Step 2: **Where?**	Curiosity has now helped you find a little space between you and the guilt or other emotion. Notice the position of your reaction? Is it somewhere specific in your body, perhaps a feeling or thought in your head, or is it outside of you?	
Step 3: **What?**	What is your reaction? Is it a thought, emotion or sensation? If you can't name it at first, be okay to say 'blank'. Then roll your eyes and blink, take a deep breath and try to name it again.	
Step 4: **Half**	Observe the reaction using the breathing and eye roll cycle until the intensity of the thought, sensation or emotion is about half of where it started. (If it stays the same, that's okay too. Do three cycles and move on to Step 5.)	
Step 5: **Purpose**	Ask the reaction: If it had a positive purpose, what would that purpose be? If the purpose is a negative purpose at first, keep asking what is the positive purpose? It doesn't make it right, it's just a purpose.	

Step 6: **Brave**	Be brave, give the reaction a voice. Don't ignore it or hide from it anymore. You can't change what you don't face. As my mentor recommends: Ask silently in your mind, "If the thought, emotion or sensation had a voice, what might it say?"	
Step 7: **Gratitude**	Be grateful that you understand more clearly now. If you can't find gratitude as yet, repeat the 7 steps. For strong reactions, we may need to do the steps 2 or more times.	

Measure the intensity of the original reaction on a scale of 0-10 again (with 10 being the worst.)

If your reaction is still above a 3 on the scale, repeat the 7 steps until the reaction feels clear.

Even though Sarah has been quoted earlier in the book, as eldest I felt it was important that she shared her perception as follows. This wonderful human being lets me know every day, that I got some things right!

CHAPTER 5: WHEN CHANGE HAPPENS

Sarah's reflections

Sarah now is a wonderful mum, with Rocco and Louie at home

Being the eldest of a blended family has had its challenges. I am opinionated at the best of times and when we've had situations where I would love to speak my mind, even when not asked, I have had to learn to rephrase it to be more suited to a blended family. I have loved the expansion of the family and people are wowed when I mention I have six siblings, which I'm quite proud to say.

My children are growing up with so much love and support in their lives and I am forever grateful to our family's hard work and determination to get us to where we all are today.

I love the topic in the next chapter, it's a personal favourite — it's all about self-care and balance. Time for me and time for them is one of the greatest keys for a mum to manage the family better. When you're nurtured you've got more time and energy for the kids and others too. Let's address ways to achieve that balance.

Her intuition was her Superpower

CHAPTER 6
Time for Me, Time for Them

Self-love. How do you feel about that phrase?

Traditionally mothers have learned from generations before them to put themselves last, that 'self-love' is an uncomfortable or selfish thing to consider. Many mums don't understand what self-love is or how to put themselves first without compromising their children's care.

Many mums have learned to 'suck it up', to sacrifice their needs for the sake of the family and yet when this is done from a place of unconditional giving, it can feel joyful and rewarding. However, when the time and effort are made from the inner energy of sacrifice; resentment, exhaustion and overwhelm can simmer beneath the surface.

Unconditional giving

Tit for tat. This is a common Australian saying and what it essentially means is that if you do that, I will do this. If you get to have something, then it's my turn. Sounds fair, right? Well sure, if you're two years old.

I come across the word 'sacrifice' a lot when mums are speaking about their motherhood and care for their children. "I sacrificed so much for my kids, I sacrificed my career, my body, my life." How does it feel when you say or even think that?

Expectations for others to give and appreciate quid pro quo, with an energy of martyrdom, can simply suck your energy dry, in addition to setting yourself up for hurt and disappointment.

Case Study – Kay's Story

Kay came to see me at clinic to begin therapy because she was feeling lost and isolated. The father of her children had found another woman and after the divorce Kay had been forced to sell the family home as part of the settlement. Now she was living in a small unit by herself. Her three children lived at least two hours away, and she'd had to re-enter the workforce to cover her living expenses.

Kay was dismayed that her children weren't there for her. It had been more than five years since the divorce and they had their own families and lives established, yet she felt resentful that she'd done so much for them during their lives, including sacrificing her career and her independence, and she now felt disillusioned.

She was very sad and hurt, and didn't understand how they could abandon her. Sadly, her conduct and the undertone of comments and looks when around her adult children had somewhat alienated them and it was clear they found their mum hard to be around. It sounded as if they would only contact her on the basis of duty, not the need and want to be around her.

After working through this situation, Kay came to the realisation of how she'd built up this resentment and that her children would love to be around her if she could just be herself and give her time and energy unconditionally. As we worked through these issues, she realised that her expectations had been handed down by her own demanding mother and aunt and that this was a recipe for disaster.

It had even spilled over into other relationships with her sister and friends. Kay realised that she'd been, without knowing it or intending to, giving her love conditionally and that to open her heart and to expect nothing in return was pure. She now felt light, content and was able to savour the joy of the times she had with family.

Sometimes the act of service is simply more rewarding.

Your joy

Give yourself permission to do the things that bring you joy. Simple things that don't necessarily need to cost money. Connect with other mothers for support. When I was home having my children, I was fortunate enough to not have to work. Yes, we did without some things, however we could cover costs and give the kids what they needed and a little bit more on the one wage.

One particular joy of mine, and an activity that I valued greatly for helping me get through the early years, was the support and connection of a mothers' group. This began from a larger group when having my first baby at the pre-natal classes. We would all arrive at someone's home once a week, place all our babies on the floor on their rugs, enjoy a cuppa and cake, and laugh, cry and share our challenges. This sharing with other mums was integral for my survival and it makes me a little sad when I hear so many working mums aren't able to find a group within their limited hours outside work.

CHAPTER 6: TIME FOR ME, TIME FOR THEM

> "Social isolation can be a risk factor for postnatal depression and anxiety. So, what seems like a social outing, is actually fulfilling an important role for mothers' wellbeing by reducing maternal stress and strengthening social bonds."

This particular group kept going for years, as mums re-entered the workforce and left the group, only to have their next child and re-enter the mothers' group. The occasional girls' night out was imperative, and we could let loose, have a laugh without babies and children, and just be ourselves. No stories to tell here, what happens on girls' night out, stays on girls' night out. Needless to say, among all the ongoing pregnancies and breast feeding, there wasn't much happening other than sheer fun and escapism.

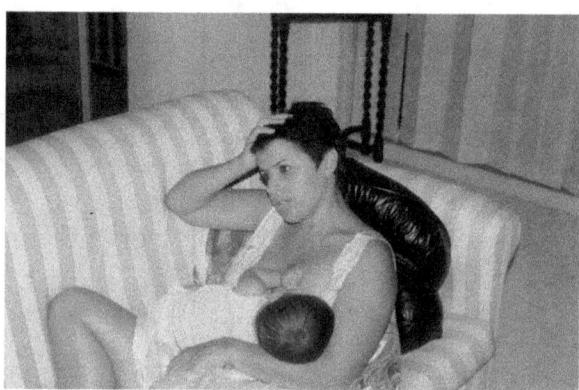

Breast feeding Gabrielle - as life went on around, this was her favourite place as a baby

Belly dancing sisterhood?

When the children were young, we lived in a large country town for a few years. We'd moved from the city to get back to grassroots for the children's dad, whose health had been suffering. For many years most of my energy had been focused on this situation, along with balancing the kids' needs, so now it was time for me to invest in some self-nourishment and connection. One of my fabulous new friends was of Lebanese origin and I was inspired when she told me of the belly dancing classes she was attending. I thought it would be a bit of fun, and at the same time a nice way of moving the body. Little did I know the connection and sheer joy I would find in this ancient art form.

Belly dancing is actually considered the oldest form of dance that was performed by women for fertility reasons or to prepare a young woman for marriage, according to BellyDance.org. Well, what do you get when you put a bunch of women together, get their bodies to express their inner wisdom and femininity and permission to loudly and shrilly express enthusiastic 'wee, lee, lees"? Sheer exultation! What I discovered is that belly dancing is about women coming together through dance and sharing their beauty and joy, as well as savouring a good belly laugh.

> *In connecting with my belly dancing sisters, I truly experienced the letting go of the 'mummy' role and was able to be present and rejoice in the essence of me, the woman!*

To quote a wonderfully acknowledged belly dancing teacher Shemiran Ibrahim, *"Through the healing powers of belly dance, a woman can start feeling more love and compassion, and become more centred, grounded and alive."*

Oxygen Mask

I often remind my mum clients of the way our air stewards used to introduce the safety procedures when showing how and when to use the oxygen mask. "This is why it's so important to put your mask on first – because without oxygen, you might not be physically capable of putting your child's mask on, let alone your own. By attending to your own first, it ensures you will have the mental and physical facilities needed to take care of your children."

Something that was highly important to me over the years, especially as a mum, was my health and fitness. I also believed it was important to lead by example — to show my children how important it is to care for yourself and stay healthy. When not working in paid employment, I would take the children to a fabulous child care at my local gym five days a week. They loved it, it was like having their own independence and friends, and I would train like a trojan. This doubled as a social connection and a form of community belonging.

It's vital to support yourself to be the best mum you can be. The importance of this for me, as an angry, testy short-fuse mum (most of the time, anyway), was apparent when the children were unwell, and I wasn't able to train. Essentially, I'd feel housebound and cranky if it was for more than a few days. Once the kids were well, I'd be straight back in to training, and calm and harmony would be reinstated. Overwhelm gets in the way of enjoying your kids, so put in place anything you need and can accomplish to avoid it at all cost.

To this day, I still train and am lucky to be attending the same gym as two of my children, as well as my husband, check out the pic here at our local gym – strong, together and having fun.

Time for me, time for them at Hiit!

When I lost my strength

In June 2013, life stressors were pretty intense. I was experiencing great sadness and was in deep overwhelm. The bank account was barely in the black, there were many mouths to feed, rent to pay to house all nine of us at the time, school fees, ballet fees etc, plus the battle for Gabby's life and her medical journey were weighing me down greatly, along with the ongoing child support battle and all the tough things that come with divorce. I found myself in great despair.

> *I simply couldn't get out of my pyjamas for weeks. I'd get out of bed, see to everyone's needs, then cower in the corner in my dressing gown, eating junk food and pretending to be working.*

There just didn't seem to be anywhere to turn, even though I had the love of my partner and the kids. I saw no way out but to go to my family GP for help. My doctor reassured me there was little wonder I was feeling like this and suggested I take antidepressants so that I could start to feel better and function in life. Regretfully, I agreed. No more than two months later I felt well enough to no longer need the antidepressants, and was able to emerge from the depression caused by the situation I was in.

At the time I wasn't a therapist and didn't have access to the funds for therapy. If only I'd known then, what I know now. Life isn't always easy and sometimes we just need a helping hand. I had to let go of my pride and give in to being 'human'. I had to learn to take some time for me.

Where are you at? Are you half full? List what gives you joy and try doing one of these each day.

Try simple things like closing your eyes and picturing yourself in your favourite place, going outside and gazing at the stars, looking at a baby photo, or taking some time to literally smell the roses, even if you have to buy them yourself.

CHAPTER 6: TIME FOR ME, TIME FOR THEM

If you feel any guilt at all about looking after yourself first or taking time for joy, use the 7 Step Formula.

7 Step Formula to let go of guilt and trust your parenting skills: Looking after self first

Step 1: **Curious**	When triggered by guilt or other disruptive emotions, get curious. If the emotion is super challenging, start by blinking three times and roll your eyes in a slow circle clockwise then anti-clockwise. (This is a concept my mentor, Maggie Wilde taught me and it works to diffuse the intensity of a reaction.) You'll be able to think more clearly and become curious about your reaction and whatever or whoever triggered you to react. Curiosity gives you the power to change your reaction.
Step 2: **Where?**	Curiosity has now helped you find a little space between you and the guilt or other emotion. Notice the position of your reaction? Is it somewhere specific in your body, perhaps a feeling or thought in your head, or is it outside of you?
Step 3: **What?**	What is your reaction? Is it a thought, emotion or sensation? If you can't name it at first, be okay to say 'blank'. Then roll your eyes and blink, take a deep breath and try to name it again.
Step 4: **Half**	Observe the reaction using the breathing and eye roll cycle until the intensity of the thought, sensation or emotion is about half of where it started. (If it stays the same, that's okay too. Do three cycles and move on to Step 5.)
Step 5: **Purpose**	Ask the reaction: If it had a positive purpose, what would that purpose be? If the purpose is a negative purpose at first, keep asking what is the positive purpose? It doesn't make it right, it's just a purpose.

Step 6: **Brave**	Be brave, give the reaction a voice. Don't ignore it or hide from it anymore. You can't change what you don't face. As my mentor recommends: Ask silently in your mind, "If the thought, emotion or sensation had a voice, what might it say?"	
Step 7: **Gratitude**	Be grateful that you understand more clearly now. If you can't find gratitude as yet, repeat the 7 Steps. For strong reactions, we may need to do the steps two or more times.	

Measure the intensity of the original reaction on a scale of 0-10 again (with 10 being the worst.)

If your reaction is still above a 3 on the scale, repeat the 7 steps until the reaction feels clear.

Meet my beautiful middle daughter. The ballerina, the academic, the organised and highly independent, Ebony. Her passion and commitment to her dance, her studies and to her friends and family are unshakable. I love her integrity and ambition to be the best version of herself. I welcome her intelligent and honest words and perception. Ebony lives interstate, however, is very connected from afar.

Ebony's reflections

My beautiful Ebony

The connotation of a separation in any aspect will always encompass a journey. In this instance, the separation of two families preceded the blended individuals we now call a family and it certainly was not the exception to the rule when it came to the battle of differing opinions, emotions, highs, lows, celebrations and often further separation. For me, this was a significant struggle as it was apparent, we were each attempting to process the change in dynamics, siblings, routines and parents while also attempting to support our loved ones.

I know I am not alone when I say the different upbringings were apparent and created many crossroads for the new heads of the household (Mum and Shane).

Now however, we look forward to the time when we are all in the same place at once (rare occasions), whether it be for notable celebrations such as Christmas, graduations and birthdays or simple Sunday morning get-togethers for fresh scones (Mum's secret recipe), jam, cream and of course coffee!

Significantly, now living interstate – you realise the benefits of having a big, always supportive and loving family which will always open the door with arms held wide for a welcome-home hug.

One family can be a handful but more and more often I hear in my clinic from mums struggling with the modern challenges of blended families. Whether it's a remarriage, or partnership, or bringing foster children into the family fold, this kind of parenting brings unique challenges all on its own. As a mum who managed the transition of a real-life Brady Bunch, in the next chapter I delve into the truth about the challenges that need to be overcome when two or more families become one.

Every Family has a story. Welcome to ours.

CHAPTER 7
The Brady Bunch Myth –
When Two Families Become One

Blended families can look quite different to each other, however, they all have similar issues.

In the late 1960s and early '70s, there was a show on television that portrayed the blend of two families, in which there was perfect balance and a happy ending for all. That improbable television show was *The Brady Bunch*.

For its time it embraced a trend that is perhaps more relevant today than it was back then. However, the show tended to sugar-coat the issues that blended families experience and, as a mum of a large blended family, the show set the bar a little high. Until I became the mum to seven kids in a blended family, I had no other example to set my expectations against.

The trouble with expectations is we are often harder on ourselves than we are on others. When *The Brady Bunch* became the basis for my experience as a blended family, it set me up to feel like I fell short.

CHAPTER 7: THE BRADY BUNCH MYTH – WHEN TWO FAMILIES BECOME ONE

> *Approximately 65% of remarriages include children from past marriages, which means the problems of a past family system sometimes cross over to a new one.*

Let's look at the blended family fantasy versus reality and get real about what to expect.

My husband Shane and I blended our families in 2012. During this time, I was still coping with fighting for Gabby's life, I had a low income and high demands of private schooling, ballet, and the expectation and desire for all our children (now seven of them) to attend university and have the best opportunities in life.

You might say this was either very brave of us or very stupid – on reflection, years down the track and now with a happy, bustling home, it was simply a little naïve. Perhaps we were looking at life with rose-coloured 'Brady Bunch' glasses. However, despite the real-life challenges that arose as a result of blending our two families, I knew then and I still know, it was the right thing to do for Shane and I, and for our amazing children.

A day of blended love, connection and fun

Would I do it all the same again?

Many things yes, however many things, no. There was no manual back then for blending a family (except perfect Carol and Mike Brady of course).

What I learned, I did so the hard way:

1. Insist on time all together. Get to know each other – eat dinner together when you can. Luckily, both our families were used to sitting down each night for dinner together. That was one of our solid commitments to ourselves and our children. It was not, of course, without its challenges;
    a. cooking for such a large tribe, sometimes as many as 8-10 at the table,
    b. and the cost and quantity to feed that many every day - a lot of spaghetti, mince, sausages and bread, and yes, I gained weight as our family grew together, but it was worth it.
    c. this time together gave us all a chance to share and get to know each other deeply. To laugh, tell stories and to connect.

One side of our big blended family was more diverse than the other in their tastes, which meant that choices in food became a compromise. One side of the family was used to eating at European times (9pm), and the other as early as 5pm for the evening meal.

Everyone had to find the happy balance, we learned to accept, adapt and we survived. In the very early days Shane's boys would often fall asleep before being called to dinner, so we

CHAPTER 7: THE BRADY BUNCH MYTH – WHEN TWO FAMILIES BECOME ONE

modified and made it work. We shared chores and helped each other out. Gabby was a terrific cook (and still is). She perfected the family shepherd's pie which became a family favourite, and there'd never be any leftovers. Lots of carbs, but we were together.

2. To add structure to our life, some rules of the house had to be enforced. For example, each family member was to text by 3pm if they weren't going to be home for dinner. Most times this worked well.

3. One rule that Shane and I chose to abide by was—be the parent not the friend. We both agreed that children deserve to have parents and a stepparent who insisted on providing structure for their children to learn and grow. There had to be guidelines and rules that were age appropriate. They needed parents, not more friends.

4. When an issue raises its head, a happy outcome is not always possible. Negotiation and compromise have to happen. Bedrooms, bathrooms, televisions, have to be shared. It's imperative to be fair and consider everyone's needs. Yes, compromise is necessary sometimes.

5. Due to the shared custody of my twin stepsons, they were with us seven days on, seven days off. At first, they had to share a room, however we managed to move to a bigger home and accommodate separate rooms for them later. We felt this was important for them to know they weren't visitors, but to have their own space equally as the other children.

6. Respect each other. Even if Shane and I had different views on some parenting skills, we agreed upfront that we would support each other when it came to how the children treated their parent or stepparent. We insisted on backing each other up to ensure that no matter whose child it was, they were to show respect to the stepparent. This didn't always happen of course; kids can only do their best and sometimes things get heated.

7. Equally, that each parent showed respect to the stepchildren. It's only natural for a parent to make more allowances for their own children, however, we agreed that we would take care not to overcompensate and make extra allowances. We would call each other out if this happened and listen to each other if someone felt compromised on this point. It really was the only way to make this work for everyone fairly.

8. Rules are to be discussed up front and then once agreed, adhered to. For example, who does the bins, washing up, mowing the lawns etc. Ownership is a great way to create family connection and a sense of fairness. Accountability for those roles according to age appropriateness is essential to build individual confidence and a feeling of contribution to the home.

Many of these guidelines were not only relevant to us as a blended family but also worked for each family prior to Shane and I joining forces.

Moments of Conflict

In dealing with the romance and new love of a relationship in the first few years, Shane and I found that we barely fought and if we did, it was only ever about the children. Based on our own individual expectations, values and house rules, we certainly didn't always see eye to eye.

At times I would make far more allowances for my stepchildren than my own biological children. I seemed to expect so much more of my kids than the stepchildren. This imbalance of overcompensation created disharmony more so in our own relationship than the children's, and sometimes still does to this day.

Be fair

Don't overcompensate by favouring your stepchildren. This is a common mistake, made with best intentions, in an attempt to avoid indulging your biological children, or vice-versa. It really is about ensuring open communication and sometimes, simply agreeing on compromise.

There was an issue that gives us all a little chuckle when we get together as a family now but wasn't quite so funny at the time. Kieran, having been very used to growing up in a house of three sisters, was quite particular with his belongings and didn't ever have hand-me-downs, or mixed up clothes. When moving in and sharing the home with three other boys, there were a few crossovers. One in particular, with his socks.

Many times, Kieran would come to breakfast and be shocked that one of the stepbrothers was clearly wearing his socks. The boys were so used to sharing and crossing over clothes, especially the twins, that they had no idea what all the fuss was about. Shane suggested a great strategy. Kieran was to mark each pair of socks differently, so that they would be matched up perfectly and branded as his.

Yes, sometimes this was overlooked by the boys, but it pretty much solved the issue.

Be alone with your child or stepchild and listen

I used to have a great system that my grown children still reminisce about.

With a young family of four children under the age of eight, I felt I wasn't able to spend enough focused time with each child individually. Sometimes one was demanding all the attention, especially with the youngest, or the child that had lots of extracurricular activities.

> *So, I devised a way that was a win-win system. I would take a child out of school for the day and spend the time doing what they wanted to do with me.*

I would alternate this one-on-one time for all my children. Sometimes it was the movies, other times a picnic, sometimes it was just hanging around home or going for a walk. Sometimes it was a shopping day just for that child. Our special days were focused individually, and I had the amazing and rare opportunity to be with that child and really give space and listen to them.

The children all loved this special time with me. Of course, it wasn't bad for them to have a break from school either ☺ but really this was paramount to me having the opportunity to check in and give each child time to breathe and feel special.

When Shane and I blended our families, we found it useful to do joint things, shake it up a bit. Perhaps have a stepchild and biological child do things together with the parents individually, or separately. We were lucky that our children went to the same school, so there was a certain history and common ground that they each shared (albeit a little weird for them at times).

I fondly recall the drive to school and pick-ups with my eldest stepson Kevin. Albeit a short drive, this was a time we had together to chat about 'stuff'. It was a normal, relaxed and comfortable time which offered a space to connect without anyone else there. I still see him in my mind, smiling with a nonchalant wave as I drove off. Spending time one-on-one doesn't need to be for long, simply a regular, enjoyable experience that adds to the memories.

Nicholas, Adam and Kevin, my gorgeous stepsons

Case Study - Be the parent (step-parent), not the friend

Within our family, we've been pretty lucky that our children, both in teenage and adulthood, have some definite high standards for respect for self and others. I believe this is partly due to the fact that we have been their parent (step) and not the friend.

CHAPTER 7: THE BRADY BUNCH MYTH – WHEN TWO FAMILIES BECOME ONE

A client of mine, Karen, presented with emotional issues, including anxiety and depression. Karen hadn't experienced a trauma at all, and she was very confused as to why she was feeling this way. After many 'talk therapy' sessions and being on medication for quite a while, she was beginning to think this was just the way life was to be.

After exploring her past, it was apparent that during her parents' separation while Karen was in primary school, her mum had used her as her confidante and told her everything that was going on, including her disgruntlement with Karen's father and the financial hardships she was suffering – all blamed on Karen's father. As a child, Karen was confused by the complexities of this but once healed within therapy, her life opened up and she was able to move forward, free of the mental health issues she'd been experiencing for so long.

> *It all comes back to the simple fact; your child is not your friend. They have plenty of friends. What they need from you is a parent who cares enough to do the tough stuff, be the adult.*

If you try to be friends with your child (before they are an adult) it comes at the cost of your authority, and it undermines your role as a parent and as Karen's case shows, confuses and burdens the child.

What if?

> What do you feel guilty about?

> What could you have done better?

> Were you listening to your intuition or perhaps listening to others outside of your trusted circle?

Here are a few of mine to start with. Consider if you had listened to your intuition, perhaps there may have been a different experience/outcome.

I feel guilty because	If I had trusted my intuition
I didn't take the time to spend with my stepsons, individually	We would have established some memories that could have strengthened our relationship and helped the boys feel more settled and connected
I didn't create enough family outings, e.g. movies, picnics	We would have even more connection and memories of the blended unit
I didn't insist on creating an open forum for us all to share thoughts and expectations before moving in together	Perhaps all the kids would feel validated and understood even more

Acknowledgement and Ceremonies

At an event I attended I was fortunate to hear a wonderful Australian Indigenous lady by the name of Deborah Sandy, of the Chepara Nation, open the event and acknowledge and perform the Welcome to the Country.

In recognising the Australian Indigenous traditional laws, I learnt from Deborah that to come onto the country of another nation (tribe's land) it's a requirement to be invited or permitted. The people wishing to enter have to wait outside the land until they are permitted in and they need someone to receive them. According to Deborah, this well-respected custom is still acknowledged and followed to this day.

I see this as an exciting basis for blending families. Too often, we simply tell the children of each family that they will be living together. I remember back in 2012, sitting around the dinner table and speaking to my children about Shane's and my decision to blend the families into the same household. At the time, we both had our own units and the children had already had quite a few dinners and shared Christmas's together, however in hindsight, I really didn't give the kids an option. It was kind of like I was 'telling them' and then selling them on the advantages. I remember having agreement and understanding from them; however, I truly feel they saw that the decision had been made, and it was best to just go along with it.

Shane did the same, and while he gave his boys the option of voicing their objections or opinions, they weren't forthcoming and so that was taken as approval.

In understanding this wonderful ceremonial law, I think that had we provided the forum to connect as a group (new tribe) and discussed and planned the best way for everyone, and made it a little special, then it may have given acknowledgement and validation to everyone's needs, and could have avoided any disharmony.

In reflection, that's another moment of guilt I need to resolve and let go of.

What have you done in the past, or not done, that leaves you with the guilt of not doing the right thing? Make your list and work through the 7 Step Formula so it can be released.

7 Step Formula to let go of guilt and trusting your parenting skills: Blending

Step 1: **Curious**	When triggered by guilt or other disruptive emotions, get curious. If the emotion is super challenging, start by blinking three times and roll your eyes in a slow circle clockwise then anti-clockwise. (This is a concept my mentor, Maggie Wilde taught me and it works to diffuse the intensity of a reaction.) You'll be able to think more clearly and become curious about your reaction and whatever or whoever triggered you to react. Curiosity gives you the power to change your reaction.
Step 2: **Where?**	Curiosity has now helped you find a little space between you and the guilt or other emotion. Notice the position of your reaction? Is it somewhere specific in your body, perhaps a feeling or thought in your head, or is it outside of you?
Step 3: **What?**	What is your reaction? Is it a thought, emotion or sensation? If you can't name it at first, be okay to say 'blank'. Then roll your eyes and blink, take a deep breath and try to name it again.
Step 4: **Half**	Observe the reaction using the breathing and eye roll cycle until the intensity of the thought, sensation or emotion is about half of where it started. (If it stays the same, that's okay too. Do three cycles and move on to Step 5.)

Step 5: **Purpose**	Ask the reaction: If it had a positive purpose, what would that purpose be? If the purpose is a negative purpose at first, keep asking what is the positive purpose? It doesn't make it right, it's just a purpose.	
Step 6: **Brave**	Be brave, give the reaction a voice. Don't ignore it or hide from it anymore. You can't change what you don't face. As my mentor recommends: Ask silently in your mind, "If the thought, emotion or sensation had a voice, what might it say?"	
Step 7: **Gratitude**	Be grateful that you understand more clearly now. If you can't find gratitude as yet, repeat the 7 Steps. For strong reactions, we may need to do the steps two or more times.	

Measure the intensity of the original reaction on a scale of 0-10 again (with 10 being the worst.)

If your reaction is still above a 3 on the scale, repeat the 7 steps until the reaction feels clear.

I had the privilege and joy of sharing in the care and the lives of my fabulously independent twin stepsons, Nicholas and Adam. It was so interesting observing the amazing connection of these strong, beautiful young men and watching them grow through their teens. We had them 50% shared with their mum and am so grateful for this.

Nicholas and Adam's reflections (it's a twin thing, they did this together!)

My beautiful twin stepsons, Adam & Nick

Being part of this blended family started out clunky and all over the place. We were a mixture of teenagers thrown into one household and amid busy school, uni, work and sport schedules we also had to invest energy into building relationships with new family members.

We took it in our stride, but a female dominated household took some adjusting to, and it was an extended process getting used to a new mother figure in our lives. Early on, we encountered stand-off like situations as we scoped out Lynne's new authority and rules, such as having to wear a shirt at the dinner table. Now as adults with separate lives, homes and families, we have come to appreciate the family gatherings that celebrate birthdays, milestones, achievements and everything in between.

In Chapter 8 I want to touch on a topic that follows directly on from blended families. It's a challenge that I hear about quite often from mums of blended families, but also from mums (and dads) who have allowed guilt to lead them down the path of 'best friend' parenting. Let's chat about the roles we play and who is the parent here?

Welcome to being a parent of a teenager.
Prepare for a large amount of eye rolling, emotional outbursts, and thoughts of running away.
And that's just the parents.

CHAPTER 8
Who's the Adult here?

Be the mother you'd want. Are you inspiring and leading your family as a good role model? Or is it, 'do as I say, not as I do'?

And also, become the partner you'd want as a partner. Be in your relationships as you would like to be treated.

While researching this book, I was led to the wisdom of the writings of Ted Parrott, Love Like That: 5 Relationship Secrets from Jesus.

---

1. *Be mindful – not indifferent – by seeing what others don't.* Be trusting and listen to your inner voice and wisdom.

2. *Be approachable – not exclusive – by moving out of your comfort zone.* It's so much easier to hide your head in the sand and ignore what's really going on. No one's a mind reader, if we don't communicate openly it's impossible to ensure everyone's on the same page. We need to say how we feel and listen to others.

3. *Be grace-full – not judgmental – by not limiting your love to people who deserve it.* Kind of sounds like unconditional love

doesn't it? So much more rewarding and kinder to those in your life.

4. *Be bold – not fearful – by speaking truthfully and risking rejection.* I wish I'd been braver in this regard with my stepchildren.

5. *Be self-giving – not self-serving – by emptying yourself for empathy.* Just as my wise mum used to say, it's 90% give and 10% take, on both sides.

So, be the parent you'd want and you can achieve the relationship you want with your child. It will also be the relationship your child needs. What examples will you be remembered for? What examples have you learned from with your parents, caregivers or grandparents? Which ones do you want to emulate and what do you try to improve upon?

Case Study

Susan came to see me wanting help to moderate her alcohol consumption, especially the drinking at night. She also believed if she could just lose some weight, she could then exercise and that would help her sleep and she'd feel much better. Susan was worried she was setting a bad example for her early teenage daughter. We talked about her life, her busy business, and then she dropped the bomb shell.

Her foster daughter had a history of extreme trauma and neglect. Susan was being subjected to physical and mental abuse from her, so much so that she was being bruised, battered and sometimes hospitalised.

Susan loved her daughter and all she wanted was for her to be happy. She felt it would be too harsh to discipline her after all the young girl had endured.

We spoke about setting rules and being consistent to establish some certainty and structure in the home. I believe Susan experienced quite an 'ahah' moment, when I said to her, "What your daughter needs is a mother, not a friend".

I explained that children have plenty of friends, but what they desire and absolutely deserve, is to have a mother (however that looks) who understands and loves the child enough to make the effort to set boundaries, rules and ultimately, safety for them. As I spoke, I could see the relief in her eyes. She realised that she'd been overcompensating due to her daughter's biological mother's abuse.

The next time we met, Susan told me she was able to feel the strength within her and that her daughter had noticed this. The behaviour began to turn around, slowly, and Susan felt stronger in herself. She was able to feel safe in her home and enjoy her family more than ever.

Other mums I work with need to release their own childhood maternal trauma. Through therapy they are able to make sense of their own unhappy childhood and come to understand how they can turn their experiences around and be extraordinary mothers to their children.

I often reflect with these mums how lucky their children are to know that they are safe, protected and loved unconditionally. Through tackling the issues and situations of their own childhood that caused great distress and upset, these mums are ensuring the 'bad' mothering isn't repeated and enable themselves to be the very best mother they can be. Ultimately, they're teaching their children one of the greatest lessons as human beings – to learn from mistakes, failures, experiences and to grow and evolve.

When it's time to step back

I often expressed a phrase with my children and now with my parent clients of being 'age appropriate'. We as mothers take on so much responsibility for these little ones — to educate, love, share, inspire, nurture and nourish physically, mentally and spiritually. But you know, as your child gets older, you must listen to your inner voice at the same time as giving time to listen to your growing child, and allow their aspirations, hopes and dreams to replace yours.

You simply must know when it's time to put aside your ideals, views and beliefs and trust that you've done your job and it's time to hand over. This of course must be gradual. I know of some parents who see their young ones as their responsibility until they turn 18 years old, or graduate from school, and then say…you're on your own.

This also is not doing the job you are meant to do. It's the gradual letting go, of learning through experience and trial and error, and through making some mistakes that our children can confidently enter the world of adulthood with skills, resilience and knowledge.

When Gabby was a teenager and in hospital for extended periods of time, I was by her side as much as possible, being her advocate, and if not there on site I was on the phone and working in the background to ensure the very best care for her.

There were times, however, that I entrusted her to take ownership of her health. Gabby had to have nightly feeds pumped through into her GJ tube, which was through a Mic-key button in her belly. I decided that the mixing of the formula and the care and cleaning of the equipment was to be her responsibility. She accepted this, albeit a little begrudgingly, but I felt strongly that this would empower her to feel in charge of her own body and health and would work towards building her independence. It may sound harsh to some, but I knew in my heart that I needed to step back.

Grandparenting

Becoming a grandmother for the first time my life felt full of joy, wonder and excitement. Sarah, my eldest daughter, had experienced a very difficult pregnancy with sever HG (Hyperemesis Gravidarum). It was so debilitating she was unable to work or care for herself. She and her husband moved into our home temporarily, until the birth of gorgeous little Louie Charles, then moved into their own home again when he was six months old. It would have been so easy for me to step in as the experienced mother and 'take over' or even give too much advice. I had to bite my tongue many times and set myself a boundary.

This was primarily to honour Sarah and her husband Michael as new parents and to not mar their joyous time of getting to know and learn all about their new son. When Sarah was exhausted or asked for help I got to give him cuddles and certainly changed nappies often enough. I honoured this precious time, followed my intuition, and knew when it was time to step back.

To quote the extraordinary Byron Katie, speaker and author, "I can find only three kinds of business in the universe: mine, yours and God's."

Being a Nonna is one of the greatest honours of my life

Borrowed from long ago

When interviewing Deborah Sandy, of the Chepara Nation (acknowledged in Chapter 7), she shared with me the Australian Indigenous way they raise their children. As most indigenous cultures do, they have established, complex customs that have been created over thousands of years. I believe these customs are important for the western world to consider.

When the women become mothers and step into their role as the nurturer, the man's role is to hunt for food. Then, as the baby grows, the women go out and forage for the smaller food, fresh sea life, eggs, fruits and berries and nuts, while the men continue to hunt for the larger food like kangaroo and emu.

> *As the young boys grow, they watch and learn from their mothers, and then at early teenage years are handed over to the men until their early twenties, to be groomed into manhood.*

They learn to become a good hunter, able to take a wife and to raise a family. Then they are initiated into secret men's business.

Deborah believes that the reason our young ones are struggling is partly due to disconnection; the loss of community support, tribal unity, and togetherness. She believes that in the circle of life, of humanity, of Mother Earth, we need to be supported and permitted to watch and then learn from our elders so we can evolve into the adults we are meant to be.

Significantly, the boys learn from men, and the girls from women. Now, this may trigger some of you. Please know I am not suggesting we step back into the 1950s and send women back to the kitchen and the men out into the world to dominate. I'm simply suggesting that for our children to know who they are we need to ensure that we offer the teachings of father to son, and mother to daughter to enable our children to enter adulthood as strong, empowered adults. For those without biological mothers and or fathers, then same sex role models can be wonderful. Food for thought?

My moment of shame and regret

In order to preserve and protect my children's innocence and to support the appropriateness of their upbringing, I had a few major rules that I established, and the children were very well aware that they were non-negotiable.

One rule was that they were to enjoy getting to know and understand their bodies, who they were and how they looked. As such I was very strict in not permitting more than one piercing in the ears and never on the body, gentle hair colours on school holidays, and don't even talk to me about tattoos; all until they were finished their schooling. Part of the age appropriateness was to understand and get to know the opposite sex as friends, and love relationships weren't allowed, even the cute young child boyfriend and girlfriend talk, until the age of 14.

How did I come to this age as a cut off? I remember making this rule when the children were very young and I think, partly, it was because I felt I had years to go before that time and wouldn't have to deal with it until then.

My son, Kieran, was nearly 15 years old, when he told me he was pretty keen on a neighbour's daughter. She was a nice young girl, but she was only 13 years old. In hindsight, I should have left things alone and allowed the young relationship to develop as Kieran and his beau chose. To my great shame and regret, I didn't. I disallowed the relationship.

It was intrusive of me. I over-stepped my authority into Kieran's life and ignored my own rule that at 14 years old the children were allowed to have relationships. I've since apologised and he forgives me, but it doesn't make it any better.

Some things simply aren't okay. I made a huge error in judgement and behaviour and regret it to this day.

> Was I acting in the best interest of my son? Certainly not.

> Was I being true to the integrity and open communication platform that I was proud to have in the home? Certainly not.

Know when it's time to step in and know when it's time to step back and let go.

Fear, guilt and worry stop them from growing and learning their lessons. And they stop us as parents from learning what we need to know as well.

What examples are you leaving your kids with? Use the table below to list examples of what you're doing well and what you'd like to change. And if you aren't happy with who you are being, consider what you aspire to do in the future? I've given a few topics to consider, but please add as many others as you like.

How are you being the parent you'd like to be?

Are you an inspiring role model for your children?

	Where you are at now	What to change in the future
Health		
Kindness		
Being present		
Punctuality		
Self-care		
Generosity		
Structure		
Attitude to money		
Respect		

If any of your answers brought up guilt for you, remember to use the 7 Step Formula.

7 Step Formula to let go of guilt and trust your parenting skills

Step 1: **Curious**	When triggered by guilt or other disruptive emotions, get curious. If the emotion is super challenging, start by blinking three times and roll your eyes in a slow circle clockwise then anti-clockwise. (This is a concept my mentor, Maggie Wilde taught me and it works to diffuse the intensity of a reaction.) You'll be able to think more clearly and become curious about your reaction and whatever or whoever triggered you to react. Curiosity gives you the power to change your reaction.
Step 2: **Where?**	Curiosity has now helped you find a little space between you and the guilt or other emotion. Notice the position of your reaction? Is it somewhere specific in your body, perhaps a feeling or thought in your head, or is it outside of you?
Step 3: **What?**	What is your reaction? Is it a thought, emotion or sensation? If you can't name it at first, be okay to say 'blank'. Then roll your eyes and blink, take a deep breath and try to name it again.
Step 4: **Half**	Observe the reaction using the breathing and eye roll cycle until the intensity of the thought, sensation or emotion is about half of where it started. (If it stays the same, that's okay too. Do three cycles and move on to Step 5.)
Step 5: **Purpose**	Ask the reaction: If it had a positive purpose, what would that purpose be? If the purpose is a negative purpose at first, keep asking what is the positive purpose? It doesn't make it right, it's just a purpose.

Step 6: **Brave**	Be brave, give the reaction a voice. Don't ignore it or hide from it anymore. You can't change what you don't face. As my mentor recommends: Ask silently in your mind, "If the thought, emotion or sensation had a voice, what might it say?"	
Step 7: **Gratitude**	Be grateful that you understand more clearly now. If you can't find gratitude as yet, repeat the 7 Steps. For strong reactions, we may need to do the steps two or more times.	

Measure the intensity of the original reaction on a scale of 0-10 again (with 10 being the worst.)

If your reaction is still above a 3 on the scale, repeat the 7 steps until the reaction feels clear.

There's one final thing to say, and it's the purpose of this work and the drive behind what I do with the mums I treat in my clinic. What else does it take to know you are a good enough mother? Let's do this!

Trust your hunches. They're usually based on facts filed away just below the conscious level

Dr. Joyce Brothers

YOU ARE A GOOD ENOUGH MOTHER
Trust your parenting skills

**"Trust there is an answer, and the answers are always within."
Lynne Lumley**

Have you ever felt that fluttering feeling in your stomach? The kind that rises up into your chest and makes your heart race? You have to make a decision and you don't know whether that decision is exactly right or extremely wrong?

No, you're not going crazy. No, you don't have to justify these feelings. Those feelings and that reaction in your body are based on human intuition. And the impulses you experience that make you want to act on your intuition, is based on your instincts. Humans have survived millions of years, through wars, famines and even plagues, largely due to relying on intuition and instinct. However, with all the overload of opinions, knowledge and surrendering our knowing to experts, many of us have lost touch with how to consciously access that inner knowing. Sometimes that inner knowing is brushed aside as a 'silly' feeling and ignored.

In Western society, we have given our power to external sources and now find ourselves lost as to how to reconnect with our primal and innate intuition.

It is the parents

In modern society it's mothers (and fathers) who can still tap into and trust their intuition who make capable, proficient parents capable of believing in their own inner strength and resources. And who often instill those resources into their children too.

The link between a mother and child is profound and universal. Research done by Lee Nelson in the 1980s, and evidence that cells travel from the developing foetus into the mother dates back to 1893 by German pathologist Georg Schmorl, shows evidence of a physical connection that exists between a mother and child, and the connection is even deeper than anyone had previously thought.

The bond

The profound psychological and physical bonds shared by the mother and her child begin in the womb. Recent advances in molecular techniques have revealed that there is bi-directional transfer of cells between a mother and her child during pregnancy, and the presence of a mother's cells in her child, known as 'micro chimerism.'

Cells from a mother are passed on to her children, some of which are from the lineage of the mothers that have come before her. Research has even found that cells of older siblings are found in their younger siblings. Imagine that, an actual physical explanation for the connection we feel as mothers for our children and the feminine connection throughout generations. This new field of inquiry is a reminder of our interconnectedness.

It is now understood that oxytocin (the bonding hormone), endorphins, and a bevy of female hormones multiply and unite in a way that rewires your brain permanently. Most mothers understand that we don't easily lose the new neural pathways that were formed during the experience of growing that child within our body. For instance, you can't UN-remember the feel and experience of having a child. The new pathways stay, and the new hormones remain for some time. As a mother to adult children, I still experience this.

I laugh with them, I cry with them, I embrace motherhood

That fluttering feeling in the stomach and the burning within is powerful and should never be dismissed. Have you ever had that feeling? I know I have many, many times.

Case Study

A mother/grandmother came to see me in my clinic. She talked about how she was dealing with her adult daughter who'd had years of mental health issues. This mum was struggling to cope with years of worry and heartache. Sadly, her daughter had become reliant on drugs and her life was falling apart. This wonderful mum had opened her home to her daughter and child, committing most of her time and focus to support and help her daughter get back on her feet.

One fateful day, she experienced such overwhelming panic and 'knew' that something was wrong. She felt it in her bones, in her very gut. Soon afterward she discovered her daughter had unintentionally overdosed. Thank goodness her daughter survived.

A mother knows

I believe we, as mothers, have an innate knowing. I believe that at any time things aren't working, we are either not listening or do not know how to hear, not in tune OR we're on a precipice of finding a solution to a challenge we have been pondering.

When I eventually discovered the name of Gabby's illness (Rumination Syndrome) online, I experienced an actual physical surge. It was the sensation that I can only describe as a buzz, it coursed through my veins, adrenalin pumping through my body. It was such a physical and cellular inner knowing that there was no mistaking it. I absolutely knew this feeling. I knew this was the truth. I remembered the feeling from many times before. I trusted it.

These are the moments that we cannot deny as mothers. We can't deny the instinctive Mumma Bear syndrome. "Get out of my way," it says. "I'm coming through. Don't mess with me, I will fight you until you listen. Because I know how vital it is to save a life."

As I began planning and writing this book based on my journey as a mum, I realised I would often tell myself through the years that I was an audacious mum! And yet, I didn't really believe it much of the time.

In part I wrote this book to tell the story of getting my youngest daughter Gabrielle through chronic illness, having her taken away and locked up in the mental health ward, being misdiagnosed, misunderstood and having to battle the mainstream health and mental health clinicians and laws. We were literally fighting for her life, many times told she was not going to make it.

Lost jobs, lost friends, being at the very pit of despair in not knowing how to help her, to then find the answers, then to have to fight to get anyone to listen and work with to get her through this. Most of her high school years were spent in emergency departments, hospitals and in operating theatres.

It was imperative to get across the injustice and the misunderstanding in order to share and inspire other mothers to always trust their intuition and their strength first and foremost. To remember that they grew this child if not physically, then emotionally. They love unconditionally, they know!

All four of my biological children have had health issues that have been carelessly misdiagnosed and mistreated. I had to keep pushing on to find a solution.

- **Sarah** — five years of desperate poor health, suspected tonsillitis, in hospital on morphine for pain seven times, almost looking anorexic, finally diagnosed with Quincy and rushed into surgery to rectify and heal.
- **Kieran** — as a one year old with septic arthritis in his hip. Specialists wouldn't believe he was in pain. Finally,

the orthopaedic surgeon gave in to my insistence and operated to find it was very serious. The delay of weeks nearly damaged his bones for life. In hospital in gallows traction for a week and penicillin for six weeks.

- **Ebony** — as a ballerina with a spiral fracture of the leg, operated and reset her leg and sent home too early. Serious implications and nearly lost her future as a dancer. Fought back after eight weeks in full leg plaster, physio with dance specialist for months, three times a week. Damaged the leg and foot, however she danced in Italy, and danced professionally for a year before leaving dance to study law.

- **Gabrielle** — (you already know her story) taken away from the family after too many years of being misdiagnosed with a suspected eating disorder, tricked and locked up in hospital mental health ward, placed on involuntary order of the state. We won the battle and she's now healthy and moving forward in her life.

I don't share all this with you to complain, look for sympathy, or to be patted on the back. I share all this to empower you, so that you know, as a mother, stepmother, grandmother, or foster mother that you are good enough, you are stronger than you think, and to trust your intuition…always.

Phrases and affirmations to remind you of who you are

> What you do now will be different in a year, you learn, grow and evolve. It's the stuff you don't know, until you know.

> I am exactly who and what my children need and must take care of myself so I can take care of those I love.

> What other mums do has no bearing on me or my abilities.

> It's okay if they hate me sometimes, that means I'm doing my job.

- My children will appreciate that I play with them more than they will appreciate clean floors or folded laundry.
- I am not their friend; I am their mother.
- I am doing my best.
- It's okay to need, want and take a break from my family.
- There is value in everything I do.
- My children are smart, kind and happy and they learned some of that from me.
- Whatever I do today will be enough.
- I am doing a good job.
- Taking time for me is not only okay, it's necessary.
- I can love being a mum and not like them very much, and that's okay.
- I am not everything to everyone.
- I am a good mum.
- I am good enough.

Motherhood Affirmations

You know how it can be, some days we are moving along smoothly, feeling good, just knowing we are doing great.

And then…something happens, and we have the wind blown out of our sails!

Small things, big things, it just absolutely stumps us. This is when you need to remember all the beautiful affirmations and positivity that will get you through those times. Here are a few of mine, add yours, in your own words or at least borrow them from other's wisdom to sustain and support you.

Motherhood Affirmations

A mother's intuition is always right, listen to it.

You are the best mother for your child. Your instincts can tell you what to do long before your head can figure it out.

Your children have enough friends, they need you to be the mother.

It's just easier to know it, than to explain why I know it.

Never let a doctor over-rule mother's intuition.

Just ask

Us mum's worry and question ourselves, we lay awake at night wondering, have I made the right choice, should I, could I, I shouldn't have yelled …and it goes on and on.

Amid the craziness of being the full-time working mum publishing a local magazine, running the household, feeding the kids, seeing to their drop offs, pickups, ballet, school extras, karate and supporting their studies and commitments, I was questioning whether the time I was able to spend with the kids and support their senior studies was enough.

So, I asked.

I remember driving home with Kieran in the car, after a mad dash from work to the train station to get him home and then racing back to work for another four hours, with the knowledge that I would be late home yet again.

I said to Kieran, "I'm sorry it's so busy at the moment. I just don't feel like I'm being a good mum to you and your sisters."

Bless his heart, he said very calmly, "Mum, you're a great mum and we're all good. Don't worry, there's nothing wrong."

> *This touched my heart so much and I knew that I really am a good enough mum.*

An Update on Gabby – how is she now

In her darkest days, only seven years ago, Gabby had surrendered to the illness and had resolved that the doctors were probably right. She wouldn't make it to her 20th birthday.

It is now 2020 and Gabby is 23. She's healthy, fit and audacious. Gabby has created an independent life with a new car and a good work ethic. She's travelled to Canada, New Zealand, Europe,

England, Iceland, and Thailand. She has paid and gone back to high school to graduate with a high OP of 5 (highest is 1, lowest 25) and is now studying Paramedic Science at University.

Gabby still has the fighting spirit that she has always had, however many knocks she had on the way. She is kind, generous and one of the smartest and funniest young ladies I have ever known.

Gabby was once lectured by yet another doctor in the hospital that she really must 'eat' and look after herself. I was there as her advocate and put the doctor in her place saying that Gabby, at 15 years old, knew more about how to care for her body than most adults and to never speak to her with that condescending, disrespectful, ignorant manner.

Gabby smiled smugly and knew I had her back. I am proud to say she is her own advocate now. She is strong, powerful and yet beautifully soft when she chooses. She is loving and is an amazing aunty, sister and daughter and, thank god, the universe, and all beings, she has survived the trauma.

Gabby now - Graduated, happy, healthy, strong

Gabby now - Strong, fit, healthy

From Gabby

From day dot I was always to be the baby of the family. From an early age I was to be the one that got picked on, teased and made fun of.

However, this didn't last long at all, anyone that knows me can confirm that I am full of fire and that has been proven time and time again. Being born into such a strong family, filled with great values of compassion and respect, taught me what decent human beings are supposed to be like, giving me role models to look up to through life's stages and challenges.

As a kid, I remember being given the greatest things in life; the most fun, family meals, holidays, movie nights, family Sundays and sporting events.... which were every single day it seemed.

But the most important was love, and so much of it too which in my family is unconditional. My number one supporter through life, which you can probably guess, is my mum, my Mumma Bear as I call her. The one that was always with me through the good and so much of the bad, always there with me to do everything in her power to keep me alive, breathing and still maintain strength and courage to get through all that was thrown our way.

Through all of the chaos of growing up in a big family, at the age of 13 in among being ill with regular holidays to the hospital, our two families combined. At the time it seemed to be a curse, but not too long after the death stares from me to my new siblings and stepdad, it would become an amazing, fulfilled, completely full of love, blended family. With enough support to last many lifetimes.

> My siblings were by my side in the hospital in the worst of times and all those in-between, playing Pictionary, Scattegories and of course Gin Rummy, always keeping me occupied and making me smile to distract me from the horrible nights I would lay in the hospital staring at the ceiling wondering what my life would be like the next day.

So, what do I have to say about my mother? Was she good enough?

My mother was more than I could have ever hoped for and continues to show her love and support for myself and all those around me. She is truly one of a kind.

My beautiful Gabby

LYNNE LUMLEY

Queensland Government

Queensland Paediatric Gastroenterology
Hepatology & Nutrition Services
Children's Health Queensland Hospital and Health Service

Dr Nikhil Thapar
BM(hon) MRCP FRCPCH PhD
Director

Dr Fariha Balouch
MBBS DCH FRACP

Dr Frances Connor
MBBS FRACP

Dr Looi Ee
MBBS, PhD, FRACP

A/Prof Peter Lewindon
MBBS FRCP FRACP

Dr Geoffrey Withers
MBBS FRACP

Clinic Date: 13 March 2020
Transcription Services

Ms Gabrielle Rice
5/192 Delancey St
Ormiston, QLD, 4160

To whom it May concern

Dear Sir/Madam,

Re: Gabrielle Jude Rice DOB: 12/06/1997 URN: C257539

Application to join the Australian Defence Force (ADF), ref 6323974-1

I refer to your letter to Gabrielle, dated 28/2/2020, which she provided to me for response.
This letter contains some inaccuracies, which it is important to dispel. Her previous medical condition has resolved and is no longer a threat to her health or ability to serve in the ADF. I would be grateful if you could reassess her application, as she should make an excellent candidate.

As a school age child, Gabrielle had a condition called rumination syndrome. She was cured of this years ago. She is now well.

This letter is to certify that Gabrielle is physically and mentally capable of undertaking the arduous work of military service over a sustained period of time, in difficult and unpredictable conditions, without placing herself or others at risk of injury or illness. She is not at risk of aggravating her health condition through service as it was cured years ago. She is likely to be able to render unrestricted service, from the health perspective. She is not at risk of experiencing a recurrence or long term complication of an illness or injury.

Importantly, the diagnosis of "Eating disorder requiring hospital admission and invasive treatment (PEG)" was wrong . It was a misdiagnosis, reflecting the lack of awareness of rumination syndrome amongst health practitioners. Gabrielle was wrongly admitted to a psychiatric facility, which delayed her appropriate treatment. It took years for her to be correctly diagnosed with rumination syndrome, for which she was subsequently treated and cured. Rumination syndrome is a functional gastrointestinal disorder and a habit disorder (like thumb sucking). There are specific treatment strategies which are highly effective. Due to a lack of available services, Gabrielle suffered her condition for years more than she would have otherwise. Eventually, Gabrielle underwent rumination treatment at our hospital as the first patient in Australia to do so. She was immediately cured and subsequently had her PEG removed.

This report contains confidential patient medical information. It is provided for the sole use of the intended recipient, for the patient's ongoing care and treatment and for no other purpose. The intended recipient must not copy, or disclose or distribute this report to any other person or agency without the prior approval of the author of the report or the Paediatric Gastroenterology Department, Children's Health Queensland Hospital and Health Service. Should any part of this report be considered to have use for the future management of the patient's care, that information must only be disclosed with the prior express permission of the author or the Paediatric Gastroenterology Department, Children's Health Queensland Hospital and Health Service.

P: +61 7 3068 2750

Queensland Children's Hospital
501 Stanley St, South Brisbane QLD 4101 Australia

F: +61 7 3068 3469

Army Letter from Dr Frances Connor

YOU ARE A GOOD ENOUGH MOTHER: TRUST YOUR PARENTING SKILLS

Gabrielle Jude Rice   12/06/1997   C257439

Throughout this process, Gabrielle has shown incredible grit, determination and stoicism. She continued with her education and even with her martial arts (for which she has represented Australia previously). She continued to compete in and win martial arts competitions while unwell. Since being cured, she has resumed normal life with gusto, working hard both to earn a living and also to catch up on lost educational opportunities. She is an incredibly high achieving, hard-working, down to earth and resilient young woman. Physically, she is extremely tough, having thrived despite her previously illness.

In summary, Gabrielle's "eating disorder" diagnosis was a misdiagnosis, reflecting a lack of awareness of her condition among many medical practitioners. She had a condition called rumination syndrome, which was cured years ago and is not likely to recur. During her previous health problems and subsequently, she has displayed extraordinary talent for getting on with the job, remaining positive and pushing herself to be the best she can be. She has been tested and been found to be an exceptional young person. Because of her previous illness, she is uniquely placed to contribute as an outstanding member of Armed Forces.

Yours sincerely,

Dr Frances Connor
Paediatric Gastroenterologist
Provider Number: 200832FL
Electronically signed by Dr, Frances, Connor
at 8:53 AM on 2/4/2020

Army Letter from Dr Frances Connor

Thank you to all my children

Throughout the journey of writing this book, my children were asked to give a few words from their experience, views of me as a mother and their reflections on being part of this crazy tribe of ours.

I made it very clear, I would not edit their words and it was to be okay to say good and bad things. To benefit the purpose of the book for the readers, it had to be real, not looking through rose-coloured glasses and saying things that could only be found in what my down to earth hubby would say…social media smoke and mirrors!

As you may have noticed, they have been honest, sometimes bordering on challenging my sense of who I am as a woman and mother. However, I appreciate and honour their honesty and truth and now through all of this, that I am learning I really am a good enough mother.

But if I ever forget or if I find something is niggling at me I can always turn to the 7 Steps to help me remember that I am a good enough mother, and so can you.

7 Step Formula to let go of 'not good enough'

Step 1: **Curious**	When triggered by guilt or other disruptive emotions, get curious. If the emotion is super challenging, start by blinking three times and roll your eyes in a slow circle clockwise then anti-clockwise. (This is a concept my mentor, Maggie Wilde taught me and it works to diffuse the intensity of a reaction.) You'll be able to think more clearly and become curious about your reaction and whatever or whoever triggered you to react. Curiosity gives you the power to change your reaction.
Step 2: **Where?**	Curiosity has now helped you find a little space between you and the guilt or other emotion. Notice the position of your reaction? Is it somewhere specific in your body, perhaps a feeling or thought in your head, or is it outside of you?
Step 3: **What?**	What is your reaction? Is it a thought, emotion or sensation? If you can't name it at first, be okay to say 'blank'. Then roll your eyes and blink, take a deep breath and try to name it again.
Step 4: **Half**	Observe the reaction using the breathing and eye roll cycle until the intensity of the thought, sensation or emotion is about half of where it started. (If it stays the same, that's ok too. Do three cycles and move on to Step 5.)
Step 5: **Purpose**	Ask the reaction: If it had a positive purpose, what would that purpose be? If the purpose is a negative purpose at first, keep asking what is the positive purpose? It doesn't make it right, it's just a purpose.

Step 6: **Brave**		Be brave, give the reaction a voice. Don't ignore it or hide from it anymore. You can't change what you don't face. As my mentor recommends: Ask silently in your mind, "If the thought, emotion or sensation had a voice, what might it say?"
Step 7: **Gratitude**		Be grateful that you understand more clearly now. If you can't find gratitude as yet, repeat the 7 Steps. For strong reactions, we may need to do the steps two or more times.

Measure the intensity of the original reaction on a scale of 0-10 again (with 10 being the worst.)

If your reaction is still above a 3 on the scale, repeat the 7 steps until the reaction feels clear.

ACKNOWLEDGEMENTS

To my beautiful daughter **Gabby.** Thank you for letting me share your story. If not for your generosity, your fighting spirit, your love and kindness, I could not have created this publication of which I know will grow and spread the word, ultimately to save others from the hell that you were put through.

"They know me in a way no one else ever has, they open me to things I never knew existed, they drive me to insanity, push me to my depths. They are the beat of my heart, pulse in my veins and the energy in my soul. They are my children"… **Sarah, Kieran, Ebony, Gabrielle, Kevin, Nicholas, Adam.**

My love, my heart, my husband, **Shane.** You have been my soft place to fall, the space for me to hide away and cry and scream, the strength when I felt I couldn't keep going. You held the belief in me when I was low and you were the quiet, never ending voice in my heart.

To **Michael,** my gentle, loving son-in-law. For your love and support, for being there for Gabby as you became part of our family. Not because you had to, but because you chose to love and care for her. Thank you for being the clown to make her laugh, the arms to hold her when she was sad and most of all, for giving in union with Sarah, our beautiful grandsons Louie and Rocco.

ACKNOWLEDGEMENTS

Dr Frances Connor of whom I will be forever indebted for the patience, the expertise and the ultimate care that saved my beautiful Gabby's life. Frances, without your compassion and insistence that Gabby's health was the issue, there could not have been a happy ending to this tale.

To **Make-a-Wish Australia** for providing such an amazing day for Gabby when she was so ill. Your tireless commitment for children who are so sick is extraordinary. We are forever grateful.

To my mentor and Publisher **Maggie Wilde.** Maggie, from the very beginning when I shared my story and dream with you, you have supported and guided me through this beautiful, and many times soul-searching journey. Thank you for your belief in me and your love, care and expertise. I always knew this book was to be written and it is because of you that it has now happened.

Aunty Deborah Sandy of the Chepara Nation, for your generosity of time and wisdom in sharing and connecting with me as a mother, a writer. I honour your comitment to educating and speaking for your culture so articulately.

Olivia Meyer for your friendship and support. Olivia is the multi-talented designer who saw my vision and designed the book cover. She is a beautiful woman who I am blessed to call my best friend.

Karl Neilson Photography for the wonderful fun and warmth provided during my photoshoot for the cover and his sensational professionalism to know me so well and to create just what we needed.

Kim Ivanisevic Make-up for creating the natural ease of colour and dimension for the photoshoot with a brush, so that I felt beautiful.

MEET THE CONTRIBUTORS

Dr Frances Connor
Paediatric Gastroenterologist

Queensland Children's Hospital, Brisbane, Australia

Dr Frances Connor is a pediatric gastroenterologist at Queensland Children's Hospital in Brisbane. She graduated from the University of Queensland in 1990 with numerous awards including first class honours and the University medal.

Dr Connor trained in gastrointestinal motility in Australia and the United States and performs specialised motility testing for children with severe disorders of gut function. Her research in Australia and in the USA is focused on gastrointestinal motility and functional disorders.

Dr Connor initiated Australia's first specialised rehabilitation programs for children with Rumination Syndrome and works in partnership with her patients and their families.

All together, blended, messy, loving, laughing, family

My Family

Family is like music, some high notes, some long notes, but always a beautiful song.

To this beautiful family, may we be together in our laughter, our tears, our love. May we play board games into the night and may we always be together.

From Left to right: Michael and Sarah with baby Rocco, Nicholas and his lovely girlfriend Kaitlyn, Ebony, Shane, Lynne, Kieran, Adam and his beautiful new wife Jasmine, Louie, and gorgeous Gabrielle.

Maggie Wilde - The Potentialist

Therapist's Therapist, Business Development Coach and Publisher to Practitioners in the Healthcare Industry.

REFERENCES AND RECOMMENDED READING

O'Hanlon, Bill. *Do One Thing Different: Ten Simple Ways to Change Your Life.* HarperCollins Publishers Inc 2019.

Segal, Inna. The Secret Language of your Body, *The Essential Guide to Health and Wellness.* Beyond Words Publishing 2010

Wilde, Maggie. *Unleashed: How to Embrace Who You Are and Empower Yourself to Reach Your Potential - FAST!* Mind Design Centre Publishing and Black Card Books, 2019.

Carroll, Lee and Tober, Jan. *The Indigo Children, Essential Reading for all Parents of Unusually Bright and Active Children.* Hay House Inc. 1999

Dr CL Claridge. *Buddha Heart Parenting, Enrich your family with Buddhist wisdom and compassion.* Vajra Publications 2012

Day, Jennifer. *Intuitive Parenting, How to tune into your innate wisdom.* Little, Brown Book Group 2019

Viegas, Marneta. *The Magic Box, Relax Kids.* Our Street Books 1988

REFERENCES AND RECOMMENDED READING

Hari, Johann. *Lost Connections, Uncovering the Real Causes of Depression – And the Unexpected Solutions*. Bloomsbury 2018.

Williamson, Marianne. *Family Relationships*. Hay House Inc 1997

Byron Katie. *Your Inner Awakening: The Work of Byron Katie: Four Questions That Will Transform Your Life*. Simon & Schuster Audio/Nightingale-Conant 2007

Byron Katie. *A Mind at Home with Itself: Finding Freedom in a World of Suffering*. Ebury Publishing 2017.

Givens, Mark. *Lessons learned from Byron Katie and "The Work"*.

Coelho, Paul. *The Alchemist*. HarperCollins 2006.

Forssen Ehrlin, Carl-Johan. *The Rabbit Who Wants to Fall Asleep: A New Way of Getting Children to Sleep*. Penguin Random House Children's UK 2015

Biddulph, Steve. *Raising Boys: Why Boys are Different – and How to Help Them Become Happy and Well-Balanced Men*. Harper Thorsons 2003

Brown, Brene. *Daring Greatly: How the Courage to Be Vulnerable Transforms the Way We Live, Love, Parent, and Lead*. Penguin Books Ltd 2015

Dana A. Porter Ashton MACC MDiv. *Yours, Mine, and Ours: A Mother's Guide to Blending a Family (But Anybody Can Use It)*. ePUB 2018

Hart, William. *The Art of Living, Vipassana Meditation as Taught by S.N. Goenka*. Harper San Francisco 2009

Brule, Dan and Robbins, Tony. *Just Breath, Mastering Breathwork*. Simon & Schuster 2018

Thich Nhat Hanh. *The Miracle of Mindfulness*. Ebury Publishing 2008

https://www.ncbi.nlm.nih.gov/pubmed/23051901 (Accessed August 10, 2019)

https://ro.uow.edu.au/theses/843/ (Accessed August 10, 2019)

http://citeseerx.ist.psu.edu/viewdoc/download?doi=10.1.1.470.2126&rep=rep1&type=pdf (Accessed August 10, 2019)

https://www.livehealthyiowakids.org/wp-content/uploads/2017/03/Family-Mealtimes-2.pdf (Accessed August 10, 2019)

https://www.ncbi.nlm.nih.gov/pmc/articles/PMC2693961/ (Accessed August 10, 2019)

https://www.scientificamerican.com/article/scientists-discover-childrens-cells-living-in-mothers-brain/ (Accessed August 10, 2019)

https://www.scientificamerican.com/article/hormone-found-linked-to-m/ (Accessed August 10, 2019)

https://www.theatlantic.com/health/archive/2015/01/what-happens-to-a-womans-brain-when-she-becomes-a-mother/384179 (Accessed August 11, 2019)

https://www.nytimes.com/2001/06/26/health/love-anger-and-guilt-coping-with-a-child-s-chronic-illness.html (Accessed August 11, 2019)

https://www.theatlantic.com/politics/archive/2014/03/in-praise-of-polyglot-culture-and-multicultural-belly-dancing/284290/ (Accessed August 20, 2019)

http://anxietycare.org.uk/anxiety/guilt-and-shame/ (Accessed August 30, 2019)

https://www.naturalchild.org/articles/robin_grille/parent_guilt.html (Accessed August 30, 2019)

https://www.hypnosisdownloads.com/training/rewind-technique

https://www.panda.org.au/info-support/after-birth/contributing-factors-for-postnatal-depression-or-anxiety

https://www.medibank.com.au/livebetter/families/new-parents/the-hidden-benefits-of-mothers-groups/

https://www.express.co.uk/travel/articles/758140/hypoxia-definition-flight-mask

Facebook

https://www.facebook.com/agoodenoughmother/

https://www.facebook.com/RuminationSyndrome/

Links to invaluable resources and guidance

https://www.nationwidechildrens.org/conditions/rumination-syndrome

https://www.nationwidechildrens.org/specialties/rumination-syndrome-program/rumination-syndrome-treatment

https://aboutkidsgi.org/upper-gi/rumination-syndrome.html

https://theromefoundation.org/wp-content/uploads/childhood-functional-gastrointestinal-disorders-child-adolescent.pdf

http://www.giresearch.org/site/iffgd-research-awards/2013/niranga-manjuri-devanarayana

http://healthdocbox.com/Headaches_and_Migraines/66260754-Rumination-definition.html

http://healthdocbox.com/Sleep_Disorders/70757229-Teaching-diaphragmatic-breathing-for-rumination-syndrome.html

https://www.dhamma.org.au

Dr. Frances Connor – Peer reviewed publications – refereed articles:

1. Connor F. Gastrointestinal Complications of Fundoplication in Children. Current Gastroenterology Reports. 2005; 7:219-226.

2. Connor F, Rosenberg AR, Kennedy SE, Bohane TD: HBV-Associated Nephrotic Syndrome: Resolution with Oral Lamivudine. Archives of Disease in Childhood 2003 May;88(5):446-9.

3. Connor F, Angelides S, Gibson M, Larden DW, Roman MR, Jones O, Currie B, Day AS, Bohane TD. Successful Resection on Localized Intestinal Lymphangiectasia Post-Fontan: Role of 99mTechnetium-Dextran Scintigraphy. Pediatrics 2003 1 September; Vol. 112, No 3:e242-247.

4. Robertson CF, Norden MA, Fitzgerald DA, Connor F, Van Asperen PP, Cooper PJ, Francis PW, Allen HD: Treatment of acute asthma: salbutamol via jet nebuliser versus spacer and metered dose inhaler. Journal of Paediatrics & Child Health 1998 Apr 334(2):142-6.

5. Linnett V, Kim Seow W, Connor F, Shepherd RW: Oral health of children with gastro-esophageal reflux: a controlled study. Australian Dental Journal 2002 June 47(2):156-162.

6. Chang AB, Lasserson T, Gaffney J, <u>Connor F</u>, Garske LA. Gastro-esophageal reflux treatment for prolonged non-specific cough in children and adults.
Cochrane Database Syst Rev. 2005 Apr 18;2:CD004823.

7. Chang AB, Lasserson T, Kiljander, T. O, <u>Connor F</u>, Gaffney J, Garske LA. Systematic review and meta-analysis of randomised controlled trials of gastro-oesophageal reflux interventions for chronic cough associated with gastro-oesophageal reflux. British Medical Journal. 2006 Jan 332(7532):11-7.

8. Chang AB, Lasserson TJ, Gaffney J, <u>Connor FL</u>, Garske LA. Gastro-oesophageal reflux treatment for prolonged non-specific cough in children and adults. Cochrane Database Syst Rev 2006:CD004823

MEET THE AUTHOR

Lynne Lumley is a specialist Psychotherapist and Clinical Hypnotherapist. She has Accredited Advanced Diplomas in Clinical Hypnotherapy, and Psychotherapy and Neuro Linguistic Programming. She is the State Secretary of the Australian Hypnotherapy Association (AHA) in Queensland, Australia.

Lynne is the founder of Phoenix Hypnotherapy, a Brisbane based Clinical Therapy Centre helping people overcome challenges with anxiety, trauma, debilitating habits, confidence, motivation and emotional issues. Lynne empowers her clients to no longer simply survive but feel the joy of being alive.

Lynne understands motherhood from many perspectives:

As the proud mother of four, stepmother of three, and Nonna of two scrumptious bundles of joy, she knows firsthand the intricate demands that every parent, stepparent and grandparent experiences. The depth of her family's journey to come together and thrive epitomises the real life 'Brady Bunch.'

As a psychotherapist and clinical hypnotherapist, Lynne helps mothers reach that internal place that says, *"I am good enough."*

Lynne speaks regularly to parenting groups, inspiring them with tales of the real-life Brady Bunch and the depth of a mother's love to fight for the health and rights of her children.

Media

Scope (CH 7)

http://tenplay.com.au/channel-eleven/scope

Awards

Best Hypnotherapy Business of 2018

Best Hypnotherapy Business of 2019

Best Hypnotherapy Business of 2020

https://threebestrated.com.au/hypnotherapy-in-brisbane-qld

A Good Enough Mother Resources

Download free resources at
www.agoodenoughmother.com/resources

THE FAMILY GALLERY

Throughout the book I have talked about my amazing blended family… their highs and lows, joys, fears, falls and triumphs. In the editing and proofing process as this book came together, so many people commented that it would satisfy their curiosity to be able to put faces to the names and see more of the journey …

So here we go…you can call me a proud Mumma Bear, how could I resist showing off more of my beautiful blended clan.

Christmas time from Santa - Ebony Gabrielle & Kieran.

Ebony & Kieran, so close as little ones.

THE FAMILY GALLERY

Ebony's birthday, always early morning presents in bed for birthdays.

Family breakfast time. "What's that? Burnt bacon again?"

Family - we seem to laugh a lot!

Family Engagement party.

Family camping & marshmallows by the campfire.

Gabby on the right, she won the Australian title.

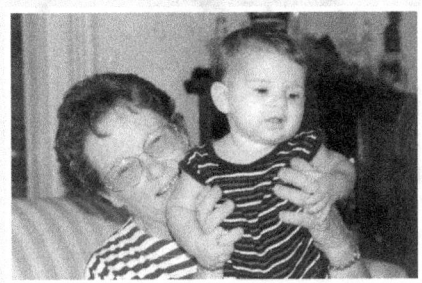

Gwenny (my mum) & Gabrielle.

Happy big sisters and brother with little Gabby.

Happy in Nanny Sue's garden.

Just messing about.

THE FAMILY GALLERY

Louie's Baby Naming Ceremony in the park - all the family.

Louie's Baby Naming Ceremony.

Sarah, Ebony, Kieran little cherubs.

The boys.

The four of them, happy and healthy kids.

The girls.

WHAT OTHERS HAVE TO SAY

"When I first started visiting Lynne, I was pregnant with my fourth child. Before every appointment with her I was suffering from a new problem physically or mentally. I left every session feeling healed on the inside and outside. Her work allowed me to care for my children and husband with confidence while going through one of the most challenging stages of my life. Without her help I would have been in so much pain and struggled with Mother's guilt tremendously. I can't thank her enough for what she has done for my family and I." **Skye Knijff, Brisbane, Australia**

"Lynne has always had such a beautiful spirit & soul. I had such an amazing, positive experience with Lynne's hypnotherapy sessions. My life was in a downward spiral with anxiety and panic attacks when just doing everyday activities. After seeing Drs and a Psychologist, Lynne suggested trying her hypnotherapy and it was a very uplifting experience. Lynne was so calming and professional in helping me work through my struggles. Sometimes I couldn't even physically get to her so we would do a Skype session. She provided me with tools and techniques to help me cope and recover. Forever grateful for all your support. xx" **Carla Cottee, NSW, Australia**

WHAT OTHERS HAVE TO SAY

"I have come to know Lynne through her hypnotherapy sessions. From our first meeting I felt instantly comfortable with her and knew I had met the right person to help me. Her caring and understanding nature has helped me greatly through several stressful situations and Lynne would be first person I would go to for help should I need it in the future. Thank you, Lynne." **Yoka V**

"I've also sent my young son for a few sessions with Lynne, he adores her and loves listening to the night-time hypno meditations. I'm grateful for her knowledge and help in my journey of life." **Sarah Dales, Redland Bay, Qld Australia**

"Lynne is kind, happy, positive and a little bit of a miracle worker. I am so blessed and happy that she has come into my life and have no problem recommending her to everyone!" **Charlotte, Yeronga Qld Australia**

"The Dr diagnosed me with PTSD and anxiety from a traumatic birth. After the first session seeing Lynne, I was around 80 % back to normal and by the second absolutely anxiety free. The deep breathing techniques I was taught from Lynne helped. I had one more consult to finalise my hypnotherapy and I was also taught meditation. I can't thank Lynne enough for what she has done. I'm so happy I don't feel that nervous anxiety for no reason and I can be a good mother, wife, and take my kids out and not feel scared about having another horrible attack. Some people suffer anxiety for decades and I conquered mine in less than a month thanks to Lynne." **Amy Duthie Brisbane Qld Australia**

"I'm now living, not just existing. Lynne has helped in a short period of time, that five years of psychiatry and medication couldn't. I cannot recommend and thank her enough." **Shyrell Nish Birkdale Qld Australia**

"After seeing Lynne, I now feel like a different person. Even friends have been commenting about how my energy is so different when I walk into the room now. I feel calmer, less emotionally charged and able to move forward in the new chapter in my life with confidence, peace and happiness. Like a weight has been lifted off my shoulders. Thank you, Lynne, for changing my life!"
Sarah Joy, Capalaba Australia

'Working with Lynne has allowed me to let go of the anxiety and pressure that I was experiencing around my desire to be the best mum to my young children. Since then, I've been able to feel so much more confident in confronting issues that make me uncomfortable, change aspects of my life that I was unhappy with, and be much, much happier all-round." **Bonnie, Ormiston Qld Australia**

"I have recently started taking my teenage son for help with addiction to video games and to help focus on his school work. After his second session he is a changed child. More focused and present in the moment instead of constantly focused on when he can play video games. I wouldn't hesitate in recommending Lynne to anyone and have referred her many times. Thanks so much Lynne for helping me with my children's health and well-being." **Belinda, Brisbane Qld Australia**

www.ingramcontent.com/pod-product-compliance
Lightning Source LLC
Chambersburg PA
CBHW070110120526
44588CB00032B/1407